Transforming the Bottom Line

Managing Performance with the Real Numbers

Tony Hope & Jeremy Hope

NICHOLAS BREALEY
PUBLISHING

LONDON

This book is dedicated to our mother, Rose,
and our wives, Pamela and Dot

First published in Great Britain by
Nicholas Brealey Publishing Limited in 1995
21 Bloomsbury Way
London WC1A 2TH

© Tony Hope and Jeremy Hope 1995
The rights of Tony Hope and Jeremy Hope to be identified as the authors of this work have
been asserted in accordance with the Copyright, Designs and Patents Act 1988.

ISBN 1-85788-102-8

British Library Cataloguing in Publication Data
A catalogue record for this book is available from the British Library.

Printed in Finland by Werner Söderström Oy

Contents

Preface

IMPROVING THE BOTTOM LINE WAS ONCE A STRAIGHTFORWARD MATTER. Managers revised strategy in the light of market changes, fixed prices based on detailed cost budgets, presented a clear business plan to which everyone could relate, and waited confidently while the organisational machine carved out another year of increased profits. But such methods no longer work. Global competition and demanding customers have changed the rules. The world of cost-plus pricing and acquiescent customers has gone for ever. Profitable customers are now hard to find and harder still to keep. The new rules of the game are innovation, speed, high quality service, and the rate at which knowledge is improved and applied. In this new world it is the commitment and contribution of the workforce which are decisive – and information the key weapon – in the battle for customer loyalty. To ignore these realities is fatal.

But, by failing to change their measurement systems, ignoring reality is exactly what most firms do. We know of many instances where the creativity, knowledge and speed of researchers and engineers have been sacrificed on the altar of cost targets. We have seen how, particularly in service industries, front-line workers are treated as costs to be minimised rather than as the ultimate expression of a firm's service philosophy and commitment. And we have seen how salespeople spend most of their time pursuing new customers with little thought as to whether their time would be better used satisfying existing ones. If it is true that behaviour is determined by what is measured and rewarded, then accounting systems have much to answer for. Designed to measure and report to shareholders, these systems cannot see behind the numbers to tell whether work adds any value. The workforce is not (and never has been) seen as an important part of the information framework.

However, finance departments have not been completely unaware of these issues. New costing systems (particularly those which are activity based) have been introduced to give managers a better understanding of product profitability, and a whole range of customer-oriented measurement systems have been adopted. But important as these initiatives are, they remain firmly rooted in a control mentality. Until managers see information as a tool to improve the business rather than a means of exercising control, they will fail to see the benefits of developing better systems.

This leads us to the main reason for writing this book. Long-term success depends on the combined efforts of managers and workers. This in turn depends on mutual trust and understanding, and a shared approach to satisfying customers profitably. To achieve these aims requires an information framework which supports and rewards good work. In our view neither traditional systems nor activity-based systems provide this framework.

We have observed a number of studies which paint a clear picture of how wasted costs can be caused. These studies begin with a listing of activities and ask whether the underlying work is relevant to the customer. By asking this question, problems which have remained hidden within traditional systems become much clearer. Moreover, because managers and workers are jointly involved in the exercise, implementation seldom entails much query or disruption. Everybody wins. Managers free up wasted time, workers feel their jobs are more secure, and customer satisfaction and loyalty are boosted.

We believe that this methodology can be formalised within what we have termed a *horizontal information system*, which monitors and reports on the value of work across the entire business. Our proposals are not derived from some secret Japanese accounting system, but Japanese managers will recognise their attributes of trust, openness, a common purpose, and a philosophy of improvement rather than control.

This book is about transforming the bottom line by providing information which binds managers and workers together in a new partnership – an essential ingredient of success in an age in which the value of organisations is based more on the knowledge and commitment of the workforce than on physical assets. Many of our key points have been made elsewhere but, like the strands of the business improvement initiatives they support, have not been brought together in a cohesive way. One of our aims is to provide that cohesion. But it would be remiss of us not to acknowledge the work of Johnson, Kaplan, Pfeffer, Meyer, Handy and Drucker.

Books are always a team effort. In particular, we would like to thank Paul Fernley whose software knowledge triggered some of the original ideas for horizontal information systems, and our publisher, Nick Brealey, for his guidance and support. And special thanks are due to Sally Yeung whose unfailing patience together with her presentation and editing skills have finally brought this book to fruition.

We expect our audience to be surprised at some of our arguments, and some readers even to be 'uncomfortable' with our more provocative comments. That is our intention. Our objective is improvement, indeed transformation, but we need to set the changes required against the background of underperforming companies and poor decision making, caused primarily by outmoded information systems.

We hope that executives, managers (particularly finance and IT managers), teachers and students of business management will all be interested in this book. Indeed, if the reaction of seminar audiences around the world is anything to go by, then issues such as how to measure customer and product profitability, how to encourage and reward value-adding work, how to measure performance, and how process teams will drive the new organisation are crucial (but largely unrecognised) elements in transforming the bottom line. We hope this book will help you ask the right questions and will lend support to your own transformation efforts.

Tony Hope   Manchester, England
Jeremy Hope   September 1995

1

THE TRANSFORMATION CHALLENGE

*Accounts can measure the results of past management, but that doesn't
add up to 'helping managers to manage' – the telling Japanese phrase
for 'management accounting'.*

Robert Heller

THE RECENT ECONOMIC TURBULENCE WITH ITS VIOLENT SWINGS IN BUSINESS
performance has challenged managerial ability as never before. With
mounting pressure to improve bottom line results, managers have relied
more and more on their accounting colleagues. But, while the ingenuity
of the finance department at preparing reported accounts knows few
bounds, their ability to support hard-pressed managers with useful
information has been less in evidence. In fact, far from helping managers
to manage, their numbers have often undermined the very programmes
on which they have based future success.

Investments in quality programmes, reengineering exercises and
team-based management structures have all been frustrated by poor
measurement systems which emphasise control rather than improvement, and low cost rather than high quality and good service. Indeed,
many of these investments are no more than acts of faith, running
alongside but not connecting with financial results. This point was well
made in a recent CAM-I report:

Techniques like total quality, reengineering, activity based costing, and empowerment are all useful tools, but each appears to address somewhat different goals and only limited aspects of performance. Ideas are colliding, not connecting. A comprehensive and unifying management approach is needed that responds to the new business environment.

Improvement fatigue is a new phenomenon. No sooner has one dose of medicine been administered than another is seen to be due. The wrong numbers are being used and the wrong options taken. This book offers a different prescription. It highlights the hidden barriers to progress and then explains what needs to be done to transform the bottom line. At the core of its agenda lies a new information system which will produce different numbers – numbers which will enable managers to eliminate huge amounts of unnecessary costs, speed up business processes, support quality programmes, improve decision making and promote innovation. These are the *real numbers*, the critical gauges which tell managers whether their actions are successful, but they are not to be found within traditional accounting systems.

Our intention is to present an alternative analysis as to why businesses underperform, and why efforts at improvement often prove to be so disappointing. There are hundreds of books that promote organisational change, but most concentrate on strategy, quality, reengineering, strong leadership, or some variation on these themes. Few recognise the crucial importance of accounting numbers and how they influence the behaviour and decisions of managers and workers. Maybe this is not surprising. Most writers on business transformation seem to assume accounting numbers to be a constant around which change takes place. We take the opposite view. We suggest that by changing the way numbers are derived and presented, management behaviour and decision making will, in turn, be radically affected. We also look at how organisations are changing and how the emerging structures urgently need new information systems. Indeed, at the dawning of the information age it is perhaps surprising to note that one aspect of business that hasn't fundamentally changed is the information system itself.

TRADITIONAL STRUCTURES, TRADITIONAL SYSTEMS

In their 1987 book *Relevance Lost: The Rise and Fall of Management Accounting,* Johnson and Kaplan exposed a significant gap between the information needed by contemporary managers and that provided by their accounting systems. They claimed that accounting information was of little help in reducing costs or improving productivity, that it failed to provide accurate product costs, and that its time horizons were too short.

Although this seminal work acted as a catalyst for the introduction of many improvement initiatives, including activity-based costing and more customer-oriented performance measures, we believe that the 'information gap' has widened. And given the speed with which the competitive climate has intensified, it's not hard to see why. The strategic buzzwords of the mid-1980s, such as total quality, fast cycle times and lean production, have fast become the accepted standards of the mid-1990s. Competitive advantage is now seen more in terms of innovation and organisational learning. What is becoming clear is that not only do accounting systems still lack relevance but, more dramatically, by providing managers with misleading signals and thus inviting the prospect of wrong decisions, they also help to destroy jobs and stifle innovation.

The forces which shape the practice of traditional management accounting are rooted in the economists' model of the firm, in which the maximisation of shareholder wealth is the overriding objective, and costs, prices and output are optimised according to the rational behaviour of rational markets. Finance managers have become expert at modelling business performance. But their models, like those of the economists, have no way of capturing quality, service, worker commitment, value creation or organisational learning. Nor, as we will argue, are they of much help to managers on more specific issues – for example whether to outsource work, how to select the least costly sales channels, or how to cut costs without damaging customer relationships. These, however, are the crucial questions that directly affect both organisations and their customers.

At one time these issues didn't seem to matter. Accounting techniques and practices evolved to serve the information needs of production-led hierarchical organisations, and they did the job exceedingly well. The reporting structure they mirror is often described as one of 'command and control' (see Figure 1.1). Bosses command and accountants control. Moreover, such ways of working are often self-perpetuating, as the CEO of Taco Bell discovered before embarking on his transformation programme:

> If something was simple, we made it complex. If it was hard, we figured out a way to make it impossible. We operated this way because with all our layers of management, we needed to make things difficult so we could keep everybody busy. The more commands and controls we had in the system, the more the system justifies its own existence.

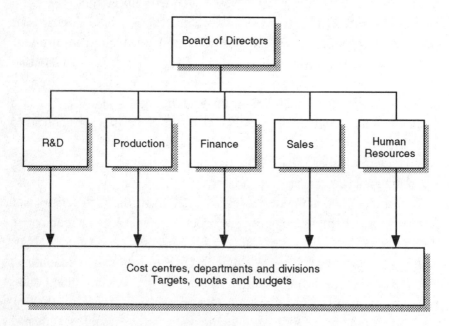

Figure 1.1 The traditional organisational structure

But these structures, and the control philosophy they promote, are fast becoming relics of a bygone era. The competitive stability which allowed organisations to plan and sell products over lengthy life cycles has disappeared. In today's marketplace, customers rule the roost and competitors can appear from anywhere at any time.

Most accounting systems fail to recognise these issues. Rather they have influenced managers into believing they can run their companies by manipulating costs, jobs and capital. They have forgotten that underneath this pyramid of numbers lie real people whose work ultimately determines the quality of products and services, and the satisfaction of customers. An excessive focus on earnings, dividends and reporting standards has obscured the real value of the work that people do.

That value must be turned into cash. The primary source of cash is satisfied customers. Satisfied customers are created by honest, hard-working people who, through their creative skills and team efforts, regularly provide customers with what they want, and they will continue to do so if they are properly recognised and rewarded for their efforts. Jack Welch, CEO at US giant GE, put it rather succinctly:

> The three most important things you need to measure in a business are customer satisfaction, employee satisfaction and cash flow.

The problem is that in almost every organisation – large and small – measurement systems say little about Welch's first two points. Phrased somewhat differently, they don't say anything about how work is done, and they don't identify which work adds value for the customer. Most accounting systems are results oriented, but are unable to tell managers *how* these results were achieved. Take, for example, the traditional variances generated by the accountant's control system. They tell managers little about the causes of their problems. They don't explain poor quality, lack of commitment or indifferent service – the information needed to compete in today's marketplace.

Given the traditional ownership view of western firms, this is hardly surprising. Shareholders put up the capital and appoint managers whose primary obligation is to account for their stewardship of these funds.

With this background it is not difficult to understand the grip of the command and control philosophy. But such a narrow view of managerial responsibility leaves many companies vulnerable to more agile competitors not hidebound with restrictive structures and systems.

CHALLENGING THE CONTROL PHILOSOPHY

Organisations develop their own 'personality' in much the same way as do people. This personality, defined by moral and ethical beliefs and codes of conduct, is also reflected in the choice of management structures, accounting systems, and the way in which people are recognised and rewarded. More often than not the organisational philosophy has stressed contractual and adversarial relationships which had one major purpose in mind – to enable the firm to compete on the basis of the lowest unit cost. Far from minimising costs, however, this philosophy has, as we shall see, often led to a growth of the very worst kind of costs – for example those relating to internal audit, contractual arrangements, business practices, and corporate governance – costs that would horrify the customer. They interfere with the real value-adding work and they slow down the critical business processes on which success depends.

Moreover, what have contracts, audits, regulations and governance to do with the building of trust and the development of common objectives between managers and workers – or the achievement of good quality, innovation, value creation, and the spreading of knowledge? And will suppliers give of their best if they must always compete purely on the basis of competitive tendering, when their alternative choice is to build long-term relationships with customers based on information sharing, flexibility, and mutual trust? But it would not be far from the truth to say that adversarial economics is built into the western business model and that, indeed, its grip has tightened in recent years. Restructuring and downsizing are both examples of this kind of contractual philosophy, and accounting systems, with their control mentality, are well positioned to carry it out.

In many ways this philosophy is strikingly similar to the 'Theory X' view of human resources set out in McGregor's classic book, *The Human Side of Enterprise*, published in 1960. Theory X stated that people hate work, need to be told what to do, and dislike responsibility. The assumption was that Theory X companies treated employees as factors of production whose output should be maximised at the lowest cost. James Baron stated the Theory X view in these terms:

> The image of the worker in these models is somewhat akin to Newton's first law of motion: employees remain in a state of rest unless compelled to change that state by a stronger force impressed upon them – namely, an optimal labour contract. Various incentive features of internal labour markets are claimed to provide forms of insurance that overcome workers' reluctance to work

The contrasting 'Theory Y' view suggested that people are motivated by self-esteem and personal development, and, thus, that companies produced better results by encouraging their people to be creative, to improve their skills, and to derive satisfaction from their work. Most managers today who proclaim allegiance to the Theory Y school would be surprised to find that the Theory X philosophy is still alive and well and living comfortably within their management structures, and their accounting and reward systems. It is rather like discovering that one section of your community still uses a language thought to be extinct.

If this seems harsh, consider the vocabulary these structures and systems use and where their reporting priorities lie. Their language is concerned with budgets, variances, standards, audits, and contracts, and their priorities are to report results to managers as fast as possible, so that this interlocking structure of performance can be monitored and controlled. They are concerned with *internal* performance and have an overarching philosophy of *control* (that's why many accountants are called 'controllers'). Words such as strategy, value-added, innovation, speed, quality and even *customer* are alien to these traditional systems.

Nor does the management behaviour encouraged by these systems seem inspiring. For example, they stifle creativity and organisational learning through a rigid budgeting system which rewards good housekeeping, but fails to acknowledge creativity or innovation; they demotivate the workforce by reporting only the cost of jobs and thus ignoring the *value of the work* people do and how well it is performed; they fail to support improvement efforts; and they continue to focus managers' attention on short-term performance by cost centre, department and division, but are incapable of measuring what's important to the customer.

Part of the problem lies in the seductive power of accounting spreadsheets. But the consequences of this 'managing by the numbers' mentality can be disastrous, particularly when applied to the annual budgeting exercise. Consider, for example, the imposition of cost constraints on the engineer who is desperately trying to meet fast time-to-market deadlines but needs more resources than the budget will allow; the production manager who wants to improve quality but has to slow down the line; the sales manager who wants to keep profitable customers longer but needs to offer short-term incentives; and the human resources manager who wants to improve the value of work through investing in the knowledge and skills of the workforce.

Undertaking each of these decisions would show a negative variance under traditional budgeting criteria, and managers would have a hard time explaining the reasons. The payback is not easily measured (indeed in most cases it is not even considered) by the accounting system. The likely result is that these decisions would not be taken in the first place.

To create the right framework for transformation, managers must think differently. They must redesign their management structures to focus on the customer, change the emphasis of their accounting and reward systems from one of control to one of improvement, and create a climate of trust and openness with the workforce by developing common purposes and sharing information. Above all, they must challenge the primacy of their financial budgeting systems, and focus their efforts on improving products, services and processes.

These changes in management philosophy were instrumental in transforming the performance of clothing manufacturer Levi-Strauss. Figure 1.2 shows how the company contrasted its old and new management beliefs.

Old Philosophy	New Philosophy
Economy of *scale* as basis for improvement logic	Economy of *time* as basis for improvement logic
Quality involves trade-offs	Quality is a 'religion' – no compromise
Doers are separate from thinkers	Doers must also be thinkers
Assets are things	Assets are people
Profit is the primary business goal	Customer satisfaction is the primary business goal
Hierarchical organisation – goal is to please the boss	Problem-solving network organisation – goal is to please the internal or external customer
Measures to judge operational results	Measure to help people make operational improvements

Figure 1.2   Levi-Strauss' management beliefs

NEW STRUCTURES, NEW SYSTEMS

Forward-thinking managers are realising how developments in technology are changing the way they manage. For example, no longer is everyone working in the same place. Indeed, 'work' is becoming less a place where people go, and more a definition of what people do. People are increasingly less constrained in their choice of workplace and they are working more with their brains than with their hands. Knowledge and service workers now dominate employment, even in manufacturing companies. And with the stockmarket value of most large companies showing a significant premium over their balance sheet values, investors have already recognised the value of these intellectual assets. Colin Maltby, CEO of Kleinwort Benson Investment Management, puts the issue this way:

> The conventional analysis of value is all about the accumulation of physical resources and physical capital. But tomorrow's sources of value, of competitive strength, are all about intangible and intellectual resources. The knowledge and skill base of the company's people, its intellectual property, its process skills, its customer franchise simply do not feature in this analysis, except in so far as they contribute to current profits.

People are becoming more mobile and are beginning to understand the value of their knowledge and skills. In short, the power base of the work-force is increasing, a change already visible within advertising firms, software companies and management consultancies. These changes are stretching the traditional control mentality to breaking point. Organisations must find new management structures that embrace notions of trust and responsibility. But to many traditional firms, this is hostile territory.

Peter Drucker explains the magnitude of the issue:

> The productivity revolution [in manufacturing] is over because there are too few people employed in making and moving things for their productivity to be decisive.....The chief economic priority for developed countries, therefore, must be to raise the productivity of knowledge and service work. The country that does this first will dominate the twenty-first century economically.

Drucker's views on the importance of productivity define much of the new competitive arena. Just as manufacturing productivity was the engine of growth throughout most of the twentieth century, so the productivity of knowledge and service workers will drive future profitability and growth. But what type of management structure will encourage this productivity growth and how will it be measured?

The emerging organisational model is the team-based structure, under which the firm is organised around a small number of key business processes. These processes encompass complete pieces of work, and their 'cross-functional' teams comprise specialists from functional departments. Many organisations have already adopted this model and have demonstrated its power by showing huge increases in productivity. Knowledge workers, in particular, seem to feel more comfortable with such structures where their work is more directly related to customer needs. However, measuring the productivity of knowledge workers is proving to be a more intractable problem.

Existing productivity measures, usually defined in terms of the number of people it takes to generate a unit of output, were designed primarily for manufacturing companies, but with manufacturing employment now accounting for less than one-third of all employees in most developed economies (and continuing to shrink), these measures are far less relevant. New productivity measures are needed in the knowledge- and information-based economy – measures which are more concerned with the value-adding content of work than simply with output per worker – but such measures present impossible challenges to traditional accounting systems.

The new team-based organisational model will succeed only if it is based on notions of responsibility and trust. Centralised, bureaucratic management systems will wither and die. And manifestations of hierarchy such as corporate headquarters, expensive inner city offices, extensive branch networks, layers of middle management, and teams of internal controllers will no longer be accepted, nor indeed necessary. In other words, as more people work from home, in project teams, on short-term contracts, or for external service providers, managers will have no option but to rethink their notions of responsibility and control. In short, they must learn to trust people. Attempts at extending traditional control systems to cover the new organisational model will undoubtedly fail, as these old ideas are increasingly challenged and rejected by more independently minded workers. Charles Handy has this to say to those managers who insist on maintaining old attitudes of control:

> Writ large, that sort of attitude creates a paraphernalia of systems, checkers, and checkers checking checkers – expensive and deadening. Some commentators have argued that audit mania is a virus infecting our society. It exists, they suggest, because we no longer trust people to act for anything other than their short-term interests. That attitude becomes a self-fulfilling prophecy. 'If they don't trust me,' employees say, 'Why should I bother to put their needs before mine?'

An organisational model built on trust also requires an information system to support it – one which binds together the interests of managers and workers and which does not alienate the workforce. The numbers in this information system won't flow from the top down or from the bottom up. Rather they will flow horizontally across the business. They can best be described as deriving from a *horizontal information system*. The design of such a system is one of the central themes of this book.

A horizontal information system is rooted in the recognition that *work* is the primary cause of costs and that the only work worth doing is that which satisfies customer needs. This is not in itself a revolutionary idea. Most workers understand it well but they have few means of knowing in practice whether their work adds value. As we have intimated, finance managers are also becoming interested. New systems which recognise that costs are caused primarily by the work people do (i.e. by their activities) are becoming popular. Activity-based systems have been heralded in some quarters as the answer to many traditional problems but, by and large, their impact has been disappointing.

It is important, at this early stage, to understand the reasons for this disappointment. Activity-based systems are usually separate from the mainstream financial information, they are typically developed in an *ad hoc* fashion, and they are project driven. They have been seen primarily as better methods of product costing, rather than as a step towards a more broadly based accounting system in which both managers and workers have an interest. In other words, activity-based systems have not challenged the control mentality and therefore have not been seen as of interest to the workforce. Horizontal systems, on the other hand, help managers and workers to measure the quality and relevance of the business processes in which they are both involved (see Figure 1.3). Indeed, one of the system's key measures – a value-adding work index – tracks the proportion of costs that adds value for customers. And by clearly identifying these costs and determing their causes, the real profits of products, customers, channels, and markets will be exposed.

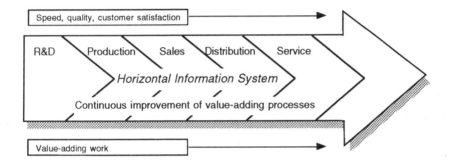

Figure 1.3   A horizontal information system

The basic questions asked by a horizontal system are simple. Does a piece of work add value for a customer? If it doesn't, why is it being done at all? And what are the causes of this unnecessary work? Why, for example, do salespeople spend so little time selling and designers spend so little time designing? If asked, most workers will admit that much of their time is spent solving problems, often caused elsewhere in the chain of transactions, which prevent them from executing their own tasks with the efficiency they would like. But what if such work could be identified and measured, and the source of these problems pinpointed and corrected? Cutting out wasted time and effort will dramatically boost the speed of process performance, which in turn will reduce costs and place firms back in the competitive driving seat.

There is strong evidence to suggest that huge amounts of work in every type of organisation add no value for the customer. Nor does this non-value-adding work relate to any particular function. It occurs equally in production departments, in research departments, in sales divisions and in administrative departments. One leading US IT vendor, for example, found that only 10 per cent of a salesperson's time was spent in front of the customer. The balance was spent progress chasing, travelling, and undertaking clerical duties. A major UK aerospace contractor identified only 20 per cent of R&D costs as being related to product development, the remaining 80 per cent being spent on meetings, documentation, and supporting manufacturing operations. In Ernst & Young's experience only 20 per cent of administrative processes add value for the customer. Many other cases will be illustrated throughout this book which present a similar picture of the significance of non-value-adding costs. *Such is their extent that their elimination would transform the bottom line of most organisations.*

These lessons were learnt long ago by Japanese manufacturers, largely from the teachings of the American quality experts Deming and Juran. Now Japanese manufacturing methods are acknowledged to be the most productive and efficient in the world. Their lean production methods, high investment, long-term perspective and low cost of capital have all been cited as crucial factors in this success. But their ability to identify and eliminate non-value-adding costs, although less trumpeted, is equally important. Japanese production workers are actively encouraged to continuously identify and root out waste. These comparisons between Japanese and western approaches have been spelt out by Johnson:

> Our management information reinforced the philosophy of controlling unit costs by producing more and faster. Their competitive philosophy, apparently not encumbered by American-style management accounting information, emphasised producing only what was demanded, always on schedule and without error or waste. They produced excellent products at low cost. We, on the other hand, failed to see that our efforts to control unit cost hampered product quality and, by causing chronic overhead creep, raised total costs.

This 'overhead creep' is often the only contact which traditional accounting figures have with the 'hidden' dimension of non-value-adding work. In other words, while finance managers might well ponder the size of these increased overhead costs appearing in the product costs and prof-it and loss accounts, their real causes are hidden from view.

SEVEN KEY TRANSFORMATION IMPERATIVES

Transforming the bottom line means different things to different people. To desperate executives and worried bankers, for example, it means fixing this quarter's results. To those managers with long-term success in mind, it means something quite different. By organising its businesses around key processes *and* measuring whether work is worthwhile, an organisation can transform its bottom line to provide increased value to all its stakeholders. This book explains these issues and suggests how new ideas can be implemented.

The agenda for this transformation process incorporates seven key imperatives. Their impact can be seen in two distinct directions. One harnesses the power of the workforce by eliminating unnecessary work, speeding up processes, improving productivity, and promoting value-creating activities; and the other shows how better management information, resulting from more relevant cost analysis and performance measurement, enables managers to improve their decision making. These issues are illustrated in Figure 1.4 in the shape of a 'transformation diamond'. The imperatives, each of which is the subject of one of the following chapters, are summarised below.

Cut the workload not the workforce

Many organisations try 'quick-fix' cost reduction programmes to improve business performance. For example, they freeze research and development expenditure or demand cost cuts across the board. As Chapter 2 explains, these short-term measures are often misguided and counterproductive. They don't address the underlying performance issues, and more often than not lead to further job cuts. Managers repeat-edly ask the wrong questions and arrive at the wrong conclusions. We

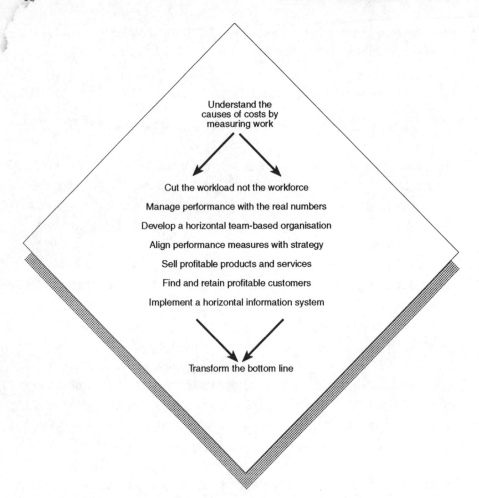

Figure 1.4   The transformation diamond

argue that managers will be able to direct their energies more effectively, from cutting jobs – the work*force* – to cutting the work*load,* by reducing work which is either irrelevant to the customer or which is performed badly. The benefits will be a more productive workforce, and an increase in long-term profits.

Manage performance with the real numbers

We believe that few managers have any real understanding of the extent of the irrelevant and poor quality work which takes place in their firms. Chapter 3 describes how various attempts have been made to identify and deal with these problems, with at best only fleeting success. We argue that only a horizontal information system can provide managers with a clear picture of organisational performance, one which allows them to improve the speed and quality of their processes by focusing their energy on the productivity of the workforce.

Develop a horizontal team-based organisation

We argue throughout that the skill, creativity and commitment of the workforce are key determinants of long-term success, but that many organisations have been slow to understand how to manage and encourage these attributes. New management structures must be developed to harness the full power of the workforce. Many organisations, realising that they have been hampered by a vertical, hierarchical structure, have begun to reorganise horizontally, based on cross-functional teams. Grouped around key business processes such as new product development or order fulfilment, the team-based approach places power and responsibility where it belongs – at the points of contact between the organisation and the customer. Chapter 4 describes the benefits which can be achieved from reorganising both reporting systems and data structures around this new model.

Align performance measures with strategy

Just as travellers need maps, compasses and charts to reach their destination (especially so if they must arrive 'on time'), so managers need good performance measures to track and encourage progress towards chosen targets. Chapter 5 discusses the choice of performance measures – those which measure attributes essential to transform the bottom line.

Who decides on the measures and how they are used are of great importance. Measures must be geared to the needs of users, whether managers of business units or team members, and must be linked firmly to strategy. To measure attributes such as speed, flexibility, innovation and price, data must cross the functional boundaries of traditional organisations, and the measures chosen must encourage the right kind of behaviour. Reward systems must support these measures and not, as so often happens, undermine them.

Sell profitable products and services

Chapter 6 looks at how managers can gain a better understanding of what their products and services must cost to be successful in markets where they have little influence over prices. It explains cost systems which stress reduction rather than control and which give a clearer view of when and where costs are incurred throughout the value chain. The emphasis is on helping managers to improve cost planning at the product's design and development stages, and to improve decision making and productivity over the product's whole life cycle.

Find and retain profitable customers

Most firms are aware of the variations in profit generated by different customers, but few realise just how many customers bring in no profit at all. Ensuring that they are able to track the costs of making products, offering services, and delivering these products and services to customers is a necessary first step in this direction, but it not enough to ensure growing long-term profits. To do this firms must retain their profitable customers.

All organisations lose customers, but few make much effort to draw them back. The factors influencing customer retention and defection vary from business to business and are often complex, but, particularly in service industries such as restaurants, hotels, airlines and banks, depend largely on perceived satisfaction with the quality of service.

Chapter 7 considers the factors which cause an organisation to lose customers and explains how retaining the right customers can dramatically increase profitability.

Implement a horizontal information system

The whole of the transformation process is underpinned by the necessity of having the right information. This isn't achievable within the traditional accounting system. To collect, analyse, track and report on issues of value-adding work and to determine the profitability of products, customers, channels and markets, requires the design of more appropriate systems. A horizontal measurement system is needed to accompany a horizontal management structure. Chapter 8 discusses how such a system can be set up and explores its potential uses.

A LONG-TERM JOURNEY

The transformation journey is more a marathon than a sprint. It requires a great deal of patience. But it is difficult to imagine how an organisation can transform its fortunes without the right information. This book argues that existing accounting systems and the management structures they support express a philosophy which is often unspecified and therefore unrecognised, but which is nevertheless pervasive. Unless these 'command and control' systems are changed, most attempts at transformation will fail.

While it is indeed our intention to attack traditional accounting systems, our arguments are also intended as a rallying cry for forward-thinking managers. We would like to place financial specialists in the vanguard of change and not, as they so often appear, as the scorers who do not partake in the game. But to take a more prominent role they must adapt their thinking to understand why processes should become the centre of organisational gravity, why the (profitable) satisfaction of customer needs is the crucial objective which ensures long-term success, and why quality, relevance, speed and value-adding performance should matter to shareholders at least as much as this quarter's results. In particular, they should understand the necessity of developing horizontal systems to follow their horizontal structures.

2

CUT THE WORKLOAD
NOT THE WORKFORCE

Given that change is inevitable, the real issue for managers is whether that change will happen belatedly, in a crisis atmosphere, or with foresight, in a calm and considered manner; whether the transformation agenda will be set by a company's more prescient competitors or by its own point of view; whether transformation will be spasmodic and brutal or continuous and peaceful. Palace coups make great press copy, but the real objective is a transformation that is revolutionary in result and evolutionary in execution.

Gary Hamel and CK Pralahad

THE FIRST PART OF THE TRANSFORMATION JOURNEY CHALLENGES THE influence of traditional accounting systems on managerial behaviour. This chapter will show how, more often than not, such systems prompt the wrong questions and, as a result, lead managers to take the wrong actions. The impact of these wrong decisions on jobs – on the workforce – can be devastating, but can be avoided when a different information perspective is taken.

CUTTING THE WORKFORCE

Many companies have reacted to the competitive threat posed by leaner and fitter organisations by hiring new strong chief executives who are experienced in 'downsizing', on the assumption that their problems are caused by falling demand which, if stabilised at a lower level, can sustain a new level of cost. The effects of downsizing are usually the same – more job cuts and more work for those who remain.

Ever since the industrial revolution, the organisational structure has been built around *jobs*. Job descriptions attempt to define the tasks that employees perform and organisation charts set out who people report to and who reports to them. Contracts of employment and a whole raft of industrial law lay down a legal framework around the definition of the job, and finance departments have evolved systems and controls to report on the costs of jobs. These systems record direct employee costs in terms of wages, benefits and taxes, and indirect costs in terms of travelling, telephoning, using buildings and supervision. The numbers and productivity of jobs are central to organisational planning and competitive analysis.

That these systems of accounting and control have seldom been seriously questioned is not surprising, as the productivity and profitability of most organisations have improved steadily throughout most of the twentieth century. But recently the wheels have come off the job-based organisation. Because accounting systems see only the cost of jobs, not the underlying work that people do, cost reduction efforts have focused on reducing the number of *jobs* rather than on the reduction of unnecessary *work*. This difference in emphasis might seem at first glance to be marginal, but it embodies the eternal truth about the real value-adding performance of most organisations – that jobs exist to serve the internal demands of the *organisation*, whereas work should only be performed if it satisfies the external demands of *customers*.

By reducing jobs, managers appear to create an instant improvement in productivity and a fall in the unit cost of output, thus creating an improving (but often illusory) picture of competitiveness. Such a unit cost mentality has had a devastating effect on the business landscape. Many large organisations have butchered their workforces in the pursuit of higher productivity and lower unit costs. In 1993, for example, large American organisations laid off 600,000 employees, a 25 per cent increase over the previous year, and the recently privatised British organisations have lost tens of thousands of jobs (in the last five years, British Telecom alone has shed 95,000) while at the same time increasing management rewards and shareholder dividends. But such programmes can all too often lead to a vicious circle of declining profits (see Figure 2.1).

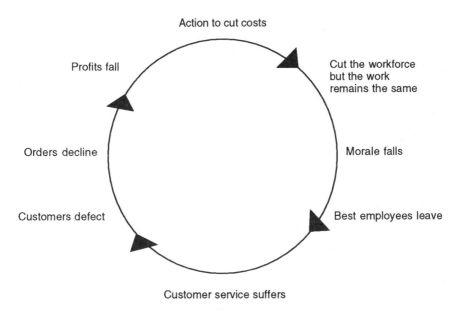

Figure 2.1   The vicious circle of declining profits

There is no doubt that cutting jobs, stretching targets and increasing rewards can offer short-term gains. But however many jobs are cut in divisions, departments and factories, the workload usually remains the same, thus throwing extra demands on fewer people and causing a downward spiral of low morale and disaffection among managers and employees, which in turn leads to declining levels of customer service and ultimately lower profitability.

Stagnant or collapsing profits, tightening cash flow, unsustainable dividend policies and a falling share price are, more often than not, the driving forces of executive action. To be seen to act is often the most important attribute – the 'acid test' of strong leadership. Like modern technological warfare, the action itself increasingly takes place on computer screens, graphs and charts. With powerful spreadsheets at their disposal, finance managers lead the attack. Their professional skills enable them to simulate business activity and forecast outcomes according to any number of assumptions. Altering a few variables changes the predicted results, and any number of 'what if?' scenarios can be inspected. Cutting costs across the board, closing a division or two, wiping out a few layers of management, or terminating a product line – each takes only a few keystrokes. But how much thought is given to the consequences of this number crunching on work flow, innovation, employee morale, management behaviour or customer service?

The answer is very little. At the first sign of problems, many executives look for swift, corrective action – a list which would probably include some or all of the following:

- ❏ setting much tougher budgets and 'stretch' targets
- ❏ demanding higher returns on all assets
- ❏ demanding cost cuts across the board (e.g. 10 per cent from each business unit)
- ❏ squeezing suppliers by tightening competitive tendering procedures
- ❏ freezing research and development expenditure, training and capital investment programmes
- ❏ cutting back overhead budgets (e.g. travel, entertaining and telephone)
- ❏ implementing 'market pricing' for internal services
- ❏ improving revenue per employee

While this type of action plan undoubtedly helps to cut certain costs in the short term, recent evidence casts doubt on its longer-term effectiveness. One recent American survey found that more than half of 350 senior managers in 275 companies (amounting to 26 per cent of US GNP) reported that short-term cost-cutting programmes had failed to meet their objectives. In another survey of 1005 companies, less than half reported meeting their cost reduction targets; 58 per cent reported that employee morale was battered; and 87 per cent that early retirement had led to the premature departure of their best employees. The poor results of improvement initiatives prompted the following comment:

> The performance improvement efforts of many companies have as much impact on operational and financial results as a ceremonial rain dance has on the weather…this rain dance is the ardent pursuit of activities that sound good, look good, and allow managers to feel good – but in fact contribute little or nothing to bottom-line performance.

Shields and Young have likened this type of 'quick-fix', short-term action programme to a rollercoaster travelling through time – where the end of the ride can be (and frequently is) a long-term failure, despite short-term thrills and successes. In the first upward rise of the rollercoaster, costs rise as the economy softens. To reduce costs, the workforce is cut. Low morale and motivational problems then lead to conflicts, shortages and delays. However, when the economy starts to improve, new employees are hired and extra costs are once again incurred in training them. Shields and Young maintain that this cycle repeats itself, but as time goes on, each new cost peak becomes higher than its predecessors:

> Lean and mean is not effective in the long term, because it attempts to reduce costs by reducing workers, but it does not reduce the work that needs to be done to make and sell products. While cutting workers, but not work, is a popular approach to traditional cost reduction, it causes an immediate decrease in costs that is usually followed by an increase because the work still needs to be done.

There is recent evidence that the second upward rise in the rollercoaster cycle has become a much bumpier ride – firms have been reluctant to rehire workers when demand picks up. Management at General Motors were allegedly astounded in 1994 when production workers went on strike because they couldn't cope with the stress caused by the extra workload, even though it resulted in large overtime bonuses. Workers demanded that extra hands be hired, but managers, with one eye on the reactions of investors, were extremely reluctant to comply.

Restructuring

When short-term cost-cutting measures are seen as mere expediency, managers often turn to some form of restructuring. In the past 10 years or so this 'corporate saviour' has generated a boom in consultancy services, but it may not necessarily be effective. Restructuring is often regarded as the stock in trade of the 'macho manager', whose maxim is 'perform or go'. It can take many forms, for example:

❑ cutting unprofitable markets, product lines and whole business units
❑ cutting management layers and driving managers harder by offering large bonuses based on the achievement of more aggressive targets
❑ stripping the business back to its core activities and selling off, closing down or outsourcing the rest
❑ combining forces with other companies (e.g. by acquisitions, mergers, strategic partnerships and alliances) and looking for substantial cost savings

These actions are taken primarily to reduce the scale of operations to realign costs with lower (more realistic) levels of sales and margins. But, because accounting systems are not designed to consider added value, managers are in a quandary – they don't know which costs to cut.

Nor do restructuring programmes address long-term competitive issues. Action taken in pursuit of the 'lowest unit cost' and the 'spreadsheet culture' of cost management have contrived to deflect managers from how work is organised and performed, and how the resources of the workforce can best be used. In short, they have failed to understand the nature of costs and how they arise; how costs can be reduced without demoralising the workforce and upsetting customers; and how their people must be treated as assets and not as mere numbers on a spreadsheet.

Without information systems which tell them what they need to know, managers are groping in the dark. The result is often poor decision making with disastrous long-term effects. Look at recent corporate history – at how once large and proud companies, and indeed whole industries, failed to respond to competitive threats which triggered a downward spiral of decline and, in some cases, self-destruction. What happened, for example, to such great western industries as motor cycles, consumer electronics, coal mining and shipbuilding? And why did so many large organisations, including Digital Equipment, Groupe Bull, IBM, Air France, American Express and British Coal, get it so wrong?

The problems faced by these organisations (and many others) don't occur only in recessionary times. They are just as real, if less apparent, in periods of economic growth. But the ebb and flow of world trade are sideshows to the main issues facing these organisations. Every customer wants to 'back the right horse' in the selection of their suppliers. Perceptions of organisational strength and management competence have risen high in the league table of customer choice. Strategic partnerships and alliances succeed only if both partners provide value and receive benefits. Organisations that are clear about their future path and demonstrate growth rather than decline are more likely to win the hearts and minds of customers and partners than are those engaged in wars of attrition within their own boundary walls.

The varying fortunes of Digital Equipment and Compaq Computer provide a vivid contrast in cost management philosophies. Throughout the 1970s and most of the 1980s Digital was one of the top performing and most innovative of American companies. Its leading-edge technology was the envy of its competitors. But in the early 1990s it fell asleep at the wheel and failed to see what was happening in its industry, which had moved rapidly towards low-cost networks, personal computing, multimedia and standardisation. Its huge investment in the high-powered Alpha chip took the company out of the orbit of most software developers.

Over a four-year period Digital cut 20,000 jobs and 10 million sq ft of manufacturing space, and saw its capital base reduce by $1.6 billion of restructuring costs. The company operated a complex matrix management structure and its products and markets were badly focused. Only when the computer systems unit was separated from the matrix did managers discover that they were losing 30 cents on every dollar of sales. Sales and administration costs were two and a half times those of one of its main competitors. In an effort to face up to its problems, Digital administered one dose of restructuring after another. It abandoned matrix management and put all its efforts into improving short-term profitability. 'The company must return to profitability in the next two quarters,' was the urgent message put out in 1994 by Enrico Pesatori, head of the computer systems division. He also identified one of the major problems facing the company when he said, 'Our engineering capabilities have become isolated from the market. We excelled in niche markets, but niche players employ 5,000 people, not 90,000.'

Digital's problems appeared to be spiralling out of control. Its attempts at restructuring weren't addressing the underlying problems of waste and inefficiency, and inadequate information systems couldn't tell managers which products, customers and markets were profitable. Therefore each series of cuts was indiscriminate in its impact. But there are signs that the new management team has recognised the problem. The number of direct customer accounts (most of which were probably unprofitable) have been cut from 10,000 to 1000, and sales through indirect channels were boosted from 38 to 50 per cent in the 12 months to June 1995. As Pesatori noted: 'We had to penetrate robust layers of management that are resistant to change.' He also acknowledged by how much Digital's costs were out of line – for example, its engineering costs were approximately twice as high as those of its rivals. Costs are now more competitive.

By contrast Compaq, after unmitigated success through the 1980s, saw premium PC prices plummet in the early 1990s and looked to be

heading along a similar self-destructive path. But in 1991 the board saw
the writing on the wall, appointed a new CEO and, with clear strategic
thinking as to where it needed to position itself in the near future, set
about creating a new company. The new management team saw that the
small business and home-user markets were about to explode on the back
of multimedia and communications, and geared its products
accordingly. 'We had to change the mindset of the whole company from
building the highest performance products in the industry to building
products that are well positioned to take advantage of the "sweetspot" of
the market at the right cost, so that we could price them aggressively,'
said Gian Carlo Bisone, VP for marketing in the USA. The chief finance
officer stressed the importance of cutting the right costs (the emphasis
was on improving manufacturing efficiency). Compaq also recognised
that its way of doing business would constantly change, for example in
its distribution strategy. According to Mr Bisone, 'We sell computers
wherever the customer wants to buy them. If they want to buy them in
gas stations, that is where we will sell them.' In the past few years,
Compaq has added to its workforce and seen its profits and share price
rise dramatically.

Compaq's recent success has much to do with its ability to go beyond
restructuring, although this has initially played its part. But many companies see business improvement as an end in itself – not merely as a
platform for future growth. Compaq's success clearly illustrates that
tomorrow's strategy may well be different from today's.

Nor are these problems confined to manufacturing firms – they have
an equal impact on banks, insurance companies, advertising firms, airlines, retailers, and legal and accounting firms. As already noted, most
cost reductions fall on people. They are increasingly seen to be the
primary cause of costs. Thus the major objective of most cost-cutting
strategies is to reduce the cost of people – often the self-same people
glowingly referred to as the source of long-term success. Whether firms
see their people as costs or assets may be the defining issue which
decides the outcome of their transformation efforts.

Consider the contrasting approaches of Sears Roebuck and Wal-Mart.
Sears Roebuck is one of America's largest and best-known retailers. But

during the late 1980s its profit record started to falter, with sales growth slipping to just 4.3 per cent per annum and operating margins falling from 4.9 per cent in 1986 to 1.2 per cent in 1990. In their attempts to reverse this decline, managers cut costs, streamlined their buying and merchandising operations and introduced 'everyday low prices'. Over 33,000 non-sales jobs were cut with projected savings of $600–700 million per annum. But managers failed to understand the real cause of Sears' problems – that poorly trained and uncommitted sales-people did not provide the level of service demanded by its traditional middle-class, middle-income customers.

The reasons for this decline in service and customer loyalty can be traced back to radical changes in the company's employment policies. From a 70/30 mix of full-time to part-time staff in the 1970s, Sears' man-agers, trying to reduce costs, reversed this balance. By the mid-1980s the mix had gone full circle (to 30 per cent full-time and 70 per cent part-time staff). But the effort in minimising staff costs proved to be the ultimate in false economy. Higher staff turnover, less training and a 'couldn't care less' attitude to employment and customer service led to a demotivated workforce, disappearing customers and declining profits.

Profits can be damaged in a number of ways. To manage a large group of part-time workers requires more supervision and controls, with addi-tional investment required in technology and security systems. Moreover, the costs of employee turnover can be far higher than most managers realise. In 1989, 119,000 jobs changed hands in the Sears Merchandise Group. The cost of recruiting and training each new employee was estimated to be $900, or $110 million in the year. This cost alone was equivalent to 17 per cent of the Merchandise Group's net profit for the year.

In 1989 Sears conducted a customer survey in 771 of its stores. The results could not have been clearer. In those stores with high staff turnover (average 83 per cent per year), customer satisfaction levels were poor, whereas in stores with relatively low staff turnover (average 54 per cent per year), customer satisfaction ratings were much higher – clear evidence of the direct correlation between staff turnover and customer satisfaction.

In contrast, Wal-Mart has grown dramatically over the past 15 years to become the most profitable large retailer in the world. A clear strategy based around sophisticated inventory management, excellent service and complete trustworthiness has proved to be very successful, and the high level of ownership by the Walton family has allowed managers to take long-term decisions without worrying about the effects on short-term results. However, the company's employment policies have been a key feature in this success. Although Wal-Mart is at the discount end of the market, it uses fewer part-time and temporary employees than any of its competitors. Local knowledge and continuity of service are acknowledged strengths of its trading policy.

Federal Express is another startling success story. The company has risen from its inception in 1973 to be one of today's top parcel carriers with around 45 per cent of the air cargo market. Its corporate philosophy is 'people–service–profit', and managers see their primary role as satisfying employee needs through job security, clarity, rewards and justice. This policy is rigorously enforced through programmes such as feedback surveys, open door policies and guaranteed 'fair treatment' procedures. The company also uses technology, including access to self-training systems, to support these policies.

Employees who perform well can expect to be promoted. Federal Express has a policy of promoting from within. It also places as much effort on recruiting lower-level employees as on higher-level ones, and looks after them well. Its employee turnover is down to 0.6% – a staggering figure compared with most companies. Moreover, those policies have led to satisfied customers – its latest survey shows satisfaction levels to be over 95 per cent.

HOW ACCOUNTING SYSTEMS UNDERMINE JOBS

It was suggested in Chapter 1 that traditional accounting systems evolved to support the command and control structure and that finance departments, charged with minimising costs, have developed sophisticated models to test their cost reduction strategies. And because employee costs represent the highest proportion of expenses in most firms, it is only natural that they become the primary target of cost reduction. This type of thinking is indicative of the 'hidden' Theory X agenda. Moreover, restructuring and downsizing programmes are the logical outcomes of this philosophy – a philosophy which often manifests itself in 'denominator' solutions to asset productivity, whether the assets are physical or human (e.g. less people rather than more output). 'Make the assets sweat even harder' and 'get more from less' are familiar expressions. And given the way that traditional accounting systems report costs (e.g. by salaries in departments), it is hardly surprising that such systems reinforce this mentality. But these systems have other, less obvious side effects which can also damage jobs.

Budgeting

We have already alluded to the pervasive influence of the spreadsheet syndrome, and how it can present managers with an illusion of reality. But such devices can only model numerical relationships, for example how profits are affected by changing prices or reducing costs. They cannot consider the impact of these changes on the remaining people.

Imagine you are the manager of an IT department which serves a range of group companies. You are about to submit the departmental budget for the following year. Cash is tight and you have been told to reduce the coming year's costs by 10 per cent. Your finance manager reckons that six jobs will have to go, but you fail to see how next year's planned work programme can be maintained without these people. Last year's expenditure and next year's budget are presented for your approval as in Figure 2.2.

Your inclination is to accept the inevitable and cut the six jobs. After all, the only alternatives are either to cut salaries rather than jobs, which would upset all the remaining staff, or to cut certain discretionary expenses, which would have only a limited effect. Before making the final decision, you ask for a different presentation of the department's costs. This is shown in Figure 2.3.

	Actual (this year)	Budget (next year)
Salaries and benefits (60 staff)	3,200,000	3,300,000
Proposed staff cuts (6 staff)	350,000	–
Travelling	900,000	800,000
Department expenses	1,050,000	900,000
Telecomms costs	500,000	400,000
	$6,000,000	$5,400,000

Figure 2.2   IT department budget

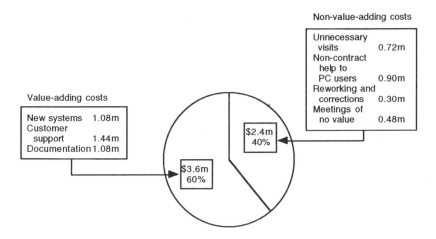

Value-adding costs

New systems   1.08m
Customer
  support   1.44m
Documentation 1.08m

Non-value-adding costs

Unnecessary
  visits   0.72m
Non-contract
  help to
  PC users   0.90m
Reworking and
  corrections   0.30m
Meetings of
  no value   0.48m

$3.6m 60%

$2.4m 40%

Figure 2.3   Re-analysis of last year's figures into the costs of work done

The revised analysis shows that the costs of activities which add value for the customer amount to only 60 per cent of last year's total – 40 per cent of the costs were caused by work which should not have been necessary in the first place. Moreover, by eliminating the causes of these costs, most of the unnecessary customer visits would be saved, and the telecommunications charges drastically reduced. These savings alone would more than cover the cost reductions demanded by head office. Looking further ahead, you can also see how the department's productivity could be improved if all this unnecessary work was eliminated.

In the light of this information, it would be surprising if your view of the budget did not radically change. Instead of cutting jobs which would damage the quality of work and the morale of the remaining workers, you would be far more likely to demand a reduction in these non-value-adding costs.

Now consider the IT manager's budget decision at a different and less challenging time. Assume now that he is requested to approve a 15 per cent uplift in the budget to cover a normal increase in business. Such an increase is in line with those of previous years. The revised figures appear in Figure 2.4.

	Actual (this year)	Budget (next year)
Salaries and benefits	3,550,000	4,150,000
Travelling	900,000	1,000,000
Department expenses	1,050,000	1,200,000
Telecommunications costs	500,000	550,000
	$6,000,000	$6,900,000

Figure 2.4   Proposed budget with 15 per cent increase

Most budgets are approved on the basis of percentage adjustments to the previous year's figures. But, given the alternative (work-based) analysis in Figure 2.3, what happens now? All the costs hidden within accounting descriptions (such as salaries and travelling), whether of value or not, are adjusted in the same way. *The result is a 15 per cent uplift in the budget for unnecessary and wasteful costs!* For example, the budget for 'unnecessary customer visits' has increased by over $100,000 and 'reworking and corrections' by $45,000. This example demonstrates that budget holders who are rewarded on their ability to stay within agreed levels have little incentive to ask searching questions concerning the strategic and work-based issues that should underpin the whole process. The net result is a huge wasted opportunity.

Because most budgets are cost based and do not deal with the *causes of costs*, no one is required to address questions of unnecessary work. This leads to the fixing of budgets in the worst possible way. 'Negotiated' cost reductions usually fall on people, and with little understanding of what people actually do, the resultant job cuts damage customer satisfaction and long-term profitability. Jack Welch, CEO of American giant GE, recently launched a blistering attack on the financial budgeting mentality:

> The budget is the bane of corporate America. It never should have existed. A budget is this: if you make it, you generally get a pat on the back and a few bucks. If you miss it, you get a stick in the eye – or worse... Making a budget is an exercise in minimilisation. You're always trying to get the lowest out of people, because everyone is negotiating to get the lowest number.

The authors of a recent CAM-I report noted that traditional budgeting techniques were being overtaken by modern management methods, 'leaving the traditional functionally based budget as an irrelevance'. Budget meetings should be a time for learning and understanding, and applying the resources of the firm to maximise its competitive advantage. But the opposite is more often the case. Why is this? Simply because managers view budgets solely as control systems, and reinforce this cost management approach with their chosen classifications and terminology.

A number of firms are becoming disillusioned with these traditional budgeting systems – largely because of the huge amounts of management time they absorb. IKEA, a large Swedish furniture retailer, is one firm that has recently abandoned its traditional systems of budgetary control. IKEA describes itself as a learning and problem-solving organisation that trusts the intuition of its staff, and this belief has led to a more informal and less bureaucratic management structure. According to CEO Andres Moberg:

We realised that our business planning system was getting too heavy; we can use the time saved for doing other things better. Now each region must merely keep within a fixed ratio of costs to turnover.

Outsourcing

As firms review their competitive strategies, they are increasingly looking to consolidate core competencies and place non-core activities in the hands of external suppliers and service providers. This devolution of work is usually known as outsourcing. In a strategic sense there is little doubt that outsourcing can improve a company's competitive position. The case for outsourcing has been put as follows:

> Thanks to new technologies, executives can divide up their companies' value chains, handle the key strategic elements internally, outsource others advantageously anywhere in the world with minimal transaction costs, and yet coordinate all essential activities more effectively to meet customer needs... Companies that understand this approach – Honda, Apple, and Merck among them – build their strategies not around products but around deep knowledge of a few highly developed core service skills. In such companies, the organisation is kept as lean as possible.

So far so good. Many companies have managed outsourcing in a strategically effective way. But the vast majority have not. The Boston Consulting Group has studied more than 100 major companies and concluded that most outsource primarily to save on overhead and short-term costs. Moreover, this results in a piecemeal approach, so there are patches of overcapacity scattered at random throughout the company's operations. This, in turn, leads to the employment of large numbers of subcontractors who are extremely costly to manage and internal departments that are individually less efficient.

In other words, most companies see outsourcing as a source of short-term cost savings (i.e. from job cuts), not as part of a longer-term strategic plan. Moreover, for many of these companies there are dangers lurking beneath the surface attractions of the outsourcing contract. Consider again the example of the IT department (Figure 2.2) with a cost structure of $6 million. Suppose now that a decision is taken to outsource the department and a bid of $5.8 million is accepted. Would this be the right decision?

It may well be if all the work of the department is covered by the out-sourcing contract. But suppose the contract did not cover the help the department was providing for its internal PC users (these have an existing support contract with a third party, but as this is only for telephone support it has proved to be totally inadequate). The work-based analysis in Figure 2.3 shows the costs of this 'hidden' support to be $0.9 million. Who will provide the help to PC users once the outsourcing contract takes effect? The answer must be that users either don't receive any support; or the firm has to pay the outsourcing company to take the extra work on; or another support contract has to be agreed with a third party. The economics of the outsourcing deal are seen in a different light.

Because most firms are organised into functional compartments, managers fail to recognise that a great deal of the work that takes place in one department is concerned with correcting errors and problems caused elsewhere. Indeed, it is not uncommon to find that the most valued employees are those who correct earlier errors and problems. Outsourcing contracts, however, are generally won on favourable comparisons with departmental costs, and with little account taken of the work which the department carries out. But, as we asked in the IT example, who will make the corrections and solve the problems once the correcters and problem solvers have gone?

The implications of such 'hidden traps' are that managers must make sure the outsourcing contract covers the whole *process* and does not simply replace the department's functional, budgetary costs. Managers often do not understand how costs are determined. Costs, or in the outsourcing example cost savings, are not always what they appear to be.

AN ALTERNATIVE APPROACH:
CUTTING THE WORKLOAD

Most businesses today are hampered in their efforts to improve profits by the way they manage their costs and their people. The opportunity to learn lessons from the catalogue of corporate failures has generally been missed – largely because managers ask the wrong questions, an approach reinforced by the orientation of their accounting systems. To complete the transformation process successfully – to move from a command and control organisation to one which emphasises teamwork, value creation, customer service and continuous improvement – requires an alternative approach, one which places strategy, innovation and the customer at the core of its measurement philosophy.

This approach poses different questions. How can business processes be improved and how can this improvement be measured? How can knowledge be harnessed and applied? How can quality and customer satisfaction be enhanced? How can profitable customers be retained over the long term? To answer these questions managers need better information systems. Although we will return to many of these questions in future chapters, one is central to our whole argument. How can firms eliminate unnecessary work? Or, phrased differently, how can firms cut the workload?

By eliminating work which does not add value, profits will improve, new investment proposals (with lower budgeted costs and higher potential returns) will become more acceptable, and more jobs will be created. A new, virtuous circle will then be created, one which increases investment, improves profits and expands the workforce (see Figure 2.5).

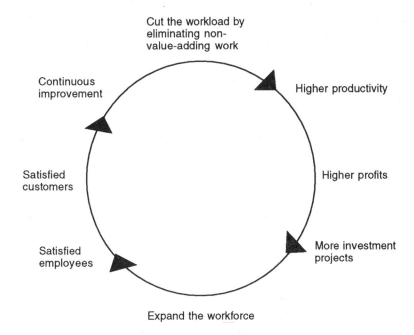

Figure 2.5   The virtuous circle of cutting the workload

How new information systems can help managers cut the workload

Many restructuring programmes focus on the rationalisation of product lines, sales channels and divisions. We have seen the impact on jobs of these decisions, which are often influenced by the presentation and classification of costs. Direct costs can readily be attributed to the revenue stream they support; indirect costs which cannot be easily attributed are 'charged' to product lines and sales channels on some arbitrary basis, usually a variant of scale or volume. In service companies, these indirect costs can be huge and thus their allocation can have a major bearing on the performance of particular product lines and sales channels.

In some organisations, finance departments have begun to use activity-based methods which charge costs according to their consumption by 'users'. However, these approaches, as Chapter 6 discusses, rarely identify non-value-adding work. The question arises as to how decisions might change if this non-value-adding work were to be quantified.

The following example illustrates how different types of information can influence a decision as to whether to close part of the branch network of an insurance company, with the loss of many jobs. The decision is viewed from three different perspectives: the traditional view of costs; the activity view; and the 'horizontal' view. It shows how a horizontal view of costs can prompt managers to ask more relevant questions, and also serves as an introduction to the concepts of a horizontal information system (a more detailed examination follows in Chapters 3 and 8).

Rocksolid Insurance Company is suffering a decline in profits. Moreover, recent legislation is about to turn the spotlight on the management costs of all insurance companies and the CEO is anxious to rationalise her company's costs before this comes into effect. Although the company has 40 branches, her attention is drawn to the four offices currently operating in one northern region. Each office has its own client base and has operated independently for over 50 years, but the advice from the strategic planning group is that only three are now sustainable. The company's accounting policy is to allocate head office costs to branches on the basis of their staff numbers.

The CEO has been somewhat circumspect about these allocations for a while and has recently requested a review of the situation. The review shows revised profit statements for the four branches. These accounts are based on an analysis of the work carried out by head office staff on behalf of the branches. But her first view of performance is provided by the traditional set of accounts (Figure 2.6).

The CEO was not surprised by these results. In fact, they were exactly in line with her expectations, and confirmed the advice she had already received – that Branch D is only marginally profitable and its operations should therefore be combined with Branch A which is only 10 miles away. Only 50 of the 150 jobs would be transferred – 100 staff face redundancy. Although this decision looks obvious, is it the right one? The CEO, having spent valuable funds on the recent review, decided to delay making her final decision until she had seen this report. The

Rocksolid Insurance Co Northern Region Profit Summary ($000s)	Total	Branch A	Branch B	Branch C	Branch D
Profit before head office costs	9,600	3,000	3,600	1,800	1,200
Head office costs	6,600	2,250	1,875	1,350	1,125
Net profit	3,000	750	1,725	450	75
Number of branch staff	880	300	250	180	150

Figure 2.6   Traditional profit summary

consultant responsible for the review began by explaining that the traditional method of allocating head office costs to branches is based on an arbitrary measure of size – staff numbers – but this measure doesn't reflect the actual use of these services. His analysis shows how the four branches have absorbed head office resources (Figure 2.7).

The consultant points out that Branch C is the real culprit – its actual use of head office resources is $1.98 million compared with an allocated cost of only $1.35 million under the old method – a reduction in profit of $630,000. Branch D, on the other hand, has made comparatively few calls on head office time and under the activity approach shows an increase in real profit of $465,000. The revised profit statement showing the results of this analysis is shown in Figure 2.8.

The branch profit picture now looks very different. At first sight Branch C seems like the obvious candidate for closure (with the loss of 180 jobs). The CEO wondered if this was the right decision. But her uncertainty was lifted when the consultant began to explain the causes of the activity costs and, in particular, which costs were of benefit to the branches and which were not. His analysis revealed the position shown in Figure 2.9.

The consultant explained that the non-value-adding costs were caused partly by poor quality work and partly by the nature of the work itself, some of which was simply not relevant to either the branch or their

Rocksolid Insurance Co Northern Region Head Office Costs (Analysed by Activity)	Total	Branch A	Branch B	Branch C	Branch D
Personnel & Training	825	330	165	248	83
Technical Support	792	317	158	238	79
Customer Support	1,320	528	264	396	132
Travel & Entertaining	990	396	198	297	99
Supervision	1,650	660	330	495	165
Meetings	1,023	409	205	307	102
Total Activity Costs	6,600	2,640	1,320	1,980	660
Traditional Analysis	6,600	2,250	1,875	1,350	1,125
Difference	0	(390)	555	(630)	465

Figure 2.7   Support costs on an activity basis

Rocksolid Insurance Co Northern Region Profit Summary ($000s)	Total	Branch A	Branch B	Branch C	Branch D
Profit before head office costs	9,600	3,000	3,600	1,800	1,200
Head office costs (activity basis)	6,600	2,640	1,320	1,980	660
Net Profit (activity basis)	3,000	360	2,280	(180)	540

Figure 2.8   Activity-based profit summary

Rocksolid Insurance Co Northern Region Analysis of Activity Costs	Total	Branch A	Branch B	Branch C	Branch D
Total	6,600	2,640	1,320	1,980	660
Value-adding costs	3,366	1,056	792	990	528
Non-value-adding costs	3,234	1,584	528	990	132

Figure 2.9   Analysis of activity costs

clients. The costs of poor quality work included ineffective meetings, non-essential branch visits, unnecessary technical support, and the excessive time taken to locate and handle documentation. The CEO realised that if these non-value-adding costs could be eliminated, the profits of the branches (and indeed the whole company) would be improved dramatically. Figure 2.9 shows the impact of removing these non-value-adding costs.

Rocksolid Insurance Co Northern Region Profit Summary ($000s)	Total	Branch A	Branch B	Branch C	Branch D
Profit before head office costs	9,600	3,000	3,600	1,800	1,200
Less: Value-adding costs	3,366	1,056	792	990	528
Real profit before non-value-adding costs	6,234	1,944	2,808	810	672

Figure 2.10   Profit summary on a horizontal basis

In fact, on this basis all four branches would be highly profitable and the original objective of lowering costs could be achieved with no loss of jobs, higher staff morale and happier clients who would not have to deal with a new office. Indeed, if the results of this analysis were applicable across the whole company, costs would be halved and profits doubled. And most jobs would probably remain in place.

This example shows how managers' decisions can be radically changed by providing better information. Instead of the decision topic being the rationalisation of branch costs, with its attendant loss of jobs, the focus has shifted to improving the flow and quality of head office work. Put a different way, the problem has moved from the branches to the head office. If branch workers don't need certain support services, or if these services are of such poor quality as to negate their benefits, then at the very least they should not be charged with them. The onus is on head office managers to improve, reengineer or eliminate the work.

A PIPEDREAM OR REALITY?

Is the notion of a horizontal system an accountant's pipedream or a realistic possibility? We are not suggesting that the downsizing programmes of recent years would have been greatly affected by this alternative approach. When the new competitive reality dawned, many companies had little option but to make drastic cuts. But *how they made those cuts* might have been radically different with more appropriate information concerning which product lines, channels and markets were really profitable.

Our approach is concerned more with long-term success. It is intended to act as a measurement framework which links the satisfaction of customers to the speed and quality of business processes, and to support the new horizontal team-based organisational model. We argue throughout this book that horizontal systems are the long-term answer to many of the problems discussed in this chapter. We show how they go beyond such project-based approaches as activity-based management and reengineering. We do not suggest that the design, development and implementation of these systems will be easy but, given current developments in information technology, such attempts are at least feasible.

The CAM-I report referred to earlier concluded that firms must base themselves on the architecture of an advanced management system – a system that links market-based strategies with operations. It suggested that such a management system might have the following parts:

❑ externally focused, market-driven targets
❑ strategy deployment driving direction and improvement
❑ focus on the outputs and effectiveness of processes and activities
❑ resource planning based on rational cost:value relationships of activities
❑ emphasis on planning, improvement and waste prevention
❑ a relevant set of performance measures
❑ simplified, flexible and responsive structures
❑ communications, teamworking and involvement

The report concluded:

> We found that even the most advanced companies do not yet have a fully integrated approach... In our view, the concepts and methods we have identified for an advanced management system provide a wide but necessary development framework in which all the components must be integrated.

The transformation agenda set out in this book offers a framework which can encompass this definition of an advanced management system. The challenge confronting finance departments is how to relate these ideas to their own business – how to create mechanisms and systems that can track costs in such a way that waste is exposed, value highlighted, and the underlying profits and losses of products and customers better explained. These issues are discussed in the next chapter.

3

MANAGE PERFORMANCE WITH THE REAL NUMBERS

Many people who have studied what the Japanese say about managing work have suggested that American managers might achieve the same goals by pursuing what is called 'activity management'. The key is to manage activities – the work people do that provides value and consumes resources. The idea is to identify the activities needed to satisfy customer wants and to compare that flow of activities with the activities presently performed in the organisation. The objective is to find and eliminate unnecessary activities now being performed and to do more of what adds value. American companies that conduct activity audits generally find that 50 to 90 per cent of the work they do adds no value to customers, although it causes a great deal of cost.

H Thomas Johnson

IT IS DOUBTFUL WHETHER THE FULL EXTENT OF NON-VALUE-ADDING WORK is properly known within any organisation. Where work audits have been undertaken, results consistently show that most organisations generate huge amounts of work for which the customer receives no benefit. The percentages of 'wasted' work vary with each particular audit, but rarely are figures of less than 20 per cent quoted. Hewlett-Packard has conducted a number of studies on this subject, some of which have involved Jim Rigby, a divisional controller at HP's South Queensferry plant in Scotland. He made this recent comment on the potential impact of reducing non-value-adding work:

> Researchers claim that most organisations have a minimum of 30% waste in their cost structure, yet typically accountants have not seen waste elimination as a major source of profit improvement. When you consider that HP in 1992 was a $16 billion company spending $8 billion in expenses, then if our wastage was 30% it represents a $2.4 billion opportunity for profit improvement. This dwarfs the impact of downsizing and the other techniques that finance directors and managements introduce.

By eliminating non-value-adding work, managers would transform the profitability of their organisations overnight. So why hasn't such a transformation occurred? Why do so many companies repeat their annual cost-reduction exercises? The primary reason is not hard to find. The measurement systems used by managers do not produce the right numbers. Managers are running their businesses with numbers designed for financial reporting and controlling budgets – purposes which have little to do with questions of adding value or customer satisfaction. But it is these questions which have everything to do with long-term success.

Organisations are successful when they execute processes speedily and without error. In the battle for customers, it is how quickly new products are brought to market, products manufactured, orders handled and customers serviced which determine winners and losers. Low levels of non-value-adding (NVA) work speed up processes; high levels slow them down. Losers are handicapped by delays, distractions, poor quality, and accounting controls which emphasise the wrong priorities. The recognition of these problems is not new, but as already suggested, most attempts at solving them have ended in failure.

This chapter argues that a *horizontal information system* provides managers with a framework within which to evaluate these problems, to understand and eliminate their causes, and thus to improve the speed and quality of business processes. At the heart of the horizontal system lies the key issue – the measurement of work – and the key question – does it add value for the customer? The extent of NVA work and its adverse effects on business performance go largely unseen by accounting systems and thus managerial demands for improvement are typically spasmodic and low key. Failure to confront these issues will represent a major error of judgement in the competitive battles ahead.

THE EXTENT AND THE CAUSES OF
NON-VALUE-ADDING WORK

The scale of non-value-adding work is hard to grasp. Different experts quote different figures. Inefficiencies, distractions, corrections, revisits, waiting and queueing all waste time and cause delays, lost opportunities and huge amounts of extra cost. No process or employee is immune. The work of designers, researchers, engineers, doctors, teachers, salespeople, production workers and accountants is similarly affected. The only question is one of degree.

An Arthur D Little survey (summarised in Figure 3.1) shows the extent and causes of the non-value-adding work of a typical engineer in an American automotive company over a one-year period. (It is little wonder that R & D engineers complain that they have so little time for creative work.)

Large amounts of non-value-adding work slow down processes and damage competitiveness. But working faster does not simply mean speeding up the current work flow. It means reviewing the way that work is done so that unnecessary work is removed and quality enhanced. As Meyer points out:

> Fast cycle time is not compressing today's activities into a shorter time frame. The only way to increase product quality and reduce cost while concurrently improving speed is to fundamentally change the process itself. Compressing the same activities into a shorter time frame without question will increase errors, escalate costs, and degrade quality.

	Value-adding	Non-value-adding
Solo work:		
Scrap or rework		10%
Valuable work	20%	
Make-work		10%
Meetings:		
Useful meetings	5%	
Useless meetings		10%
Management reviews		5%
Preparation for reviews		10%
Paperwork:		
Work documentation	5%	
Reporting for		
administrative control		
and other paperwork		10%
Communications:		
Team talk	5%	
Crisis management		5%
Miscellaneous		5%
TOTALS	35%	65%

Figure 3.1   The value-adding work of an automotive engineer

Restrictive budgets and slow approvals are a common source of delays and bottlenecks. In one US company a half-billion dollar project was six months late to market because of the delay in hiring two process engineers. The engineering group didn't hire them because it would have added $200,000 to its budget, but this delay cost the firm $10 million in lost revenue. Functional control systems are often cited as being the number one enemy of fast cycle times.

Management writers and quality consultants agree that the cost of non-value-adding work is huge, but are less in accord as to whether it can be systematically measured. We believe it can (and must) be measured, and that such a systematic approach should begin with two questions. One concerns the relevance of work: Does a piece of work add value for the customer? And the other relates to the quality of work performed: is it performed correctly first time and without delay?

Irrelevant and poor quality work

Work is said to be relevant if it provides value for the customer. But who the customer is for a particular piece of work is often far from obvious. Who, for example, is the customer of 'new product development'? Is it the manufacturing team or the sales team (i.e. 'internal' customers), or is it the (external) customer who actually buys the product? The notion of the 'internal customer' has become popular, but it can be an overused and dangerous term. Internal customers do not generate revenue; they generate costs. It is the final bill-paying consumer at the end of the entire value chain who determines whether work adds value. For example, a car parts supplier sells to a manufacturer, but the ultimate customer is the purchaser of the car. Similarly, a car manufacturer sells to a dealer, but the ultimate customer remains the final buyer. Shank has defined the value chain as:

> the linked set of value-creating activities all the way from basic raw materials through component suppliers to the ultimate end-use product delivered into the final consumers' hands.

Figure 3.2 illustrates the value chain in which one firm (Company A) forms a part. The stream of revenue from the final customer feeds the whole chain.

For work to be classed as relevant or irrelevant, it has to represent an identifiable step in a process; in other words, it must be seen as constituting an *activity*. Activities are pieces of work which consume resources; they are distinct and can (ideally) be measured. Activities are

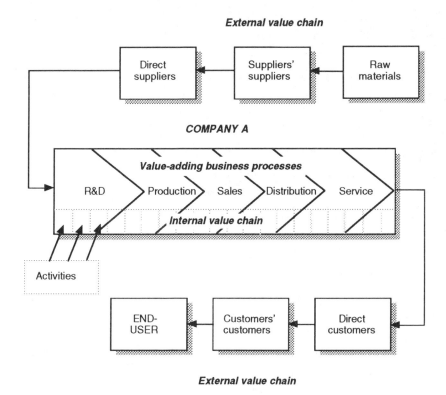

Figure 3.2   Company A's internal and external value chains

the causes and drivers of cost. Turney has noted that a typical firm has about 200–300 major activities and, by focusing attention on understanding and improving the important ones, managers will achieve maximum effect in the shortest time. He notes that Pareto's rule also applies: 20 per cent of activities are likely to cause 80 per cent of costs.

In a recent study, Hewlett-Packard defined an irrelevant activity as 'an activity which, through process improvement, can be eliminated without deterioration to the service or product'. Irrelevant activities are, however, not always easy to identify. Take, for example, work done at the testing stage during the production of a car chassis. Imagine displaying the following items on the price list in a dealer's showroom: Sun-Roof $900; Chassis Testing $90. Of course this would be laughable. How can testing add value if the customer is not prepared to pay for it? The fact is that the testing is necessary because the quality of the chassis is not good enough. The answer is to improve quality, not to expect the customer to pay.

Most large organisations, because of their fragmented departmental structures, employ people whose activities are irrelevant to the customer. This work is perhaps most prevalent in those departments such as audit, legal and administration which support the internal machinery of the company and are far removed from the customer. However, this work is difficult to remove without changing the organisational structure itself.

Sometimes, indeed, the work cannot be removed. For example, fulfilling government regulations constitutes a legal necessity. Organisations may have different 'customers' with different requirements. Work performed in satisfying these other 'customers' (government departments, environmental groups) may not directly benefit those who buy the firm's products (although in the longer run it may well do so indirectly).

Performing irrelevant (but scheduled) work can be demoralising. Nurses and teachers, for example, frequently complain about the increasing levels of interference with their primary (value-adding) duties. Meeting government regulations, filling in forms and attending meetings are an increasing part of their everyday work, but they detract from patient care, education and creativity. Drucker has noted the effects on the morale of nurses:

> This is not job enrichment; it is job impoverishment. It destroys productivity. It saps motivation and morale. Nurses, every attitude survey shows, bitterly resent not being able to spend more time caring for patients. They also believe, understandably, that they are grossly underpaid for what they are capable of doing, while the hospital administrator, equally understandably, believes that they are grossly overpaid for the unskilled work they are actually doing.

Many studies have shown the extent of irrelevant work within the production process. Miller and Vollmann, for example, have suggested that there is an entire 'hidden factory' within the more obvious physical production setting. This hidden factory, they argue, is made up of four types of transaction, none of which adds value for the customer. Thus firms:

❑ incur *logistical costs* by employing 'indirect' workers to receive, expedite, ship and account for the moving of materials between locations
❑ employ people to ensure that the supply and demand for materials, labour and capacity is in *balance*
❑ require people to ensure that transactions have taken place with the correctness or *quality* that should occur
❑ finally, and most critically in cost terms, they employ people in the 'hidden factory' simply to update their systems to account for (often multiple) *changes* in schedules, specifications of materials, and engineering designs

Activities can also be partially relevant. In other words, they can be 'rated' according to the value they provide for the customer. Activities, for this purpose, can be thought of as being divided into three categories (or 'value states'): primary (wholly relevant), secondary (partially relevant) and non-value-adding (wholly irrelevant). Take the work of a typical salesperson. His or her *primary activities* might include negotiating with the customer and taking orders – work which is directly incurred in providing value to customers and which has a 'relevance index' of 100 per cent. *Secondary activities* (such as travelling) support primary activities (such as selling), but the degree of support can vary widely. Figure 3.3 shows how an activity profile of a salesperson might appear when activities are 'rated' according to their relevance.

Analysing work by its relevance to customers is not a new approach. Consider, for example, how managers at GE approached a problem in one of their electro-mechanical assembly shops in the late 1980s. The problems arose from the poor implementation of just-in-time concepts, introduced by top management to cut costs and meet delivery schedules more consistently.

Managers began by breaking down the total manufacturing cycle time into its component activities (process, inspection, move, queue and

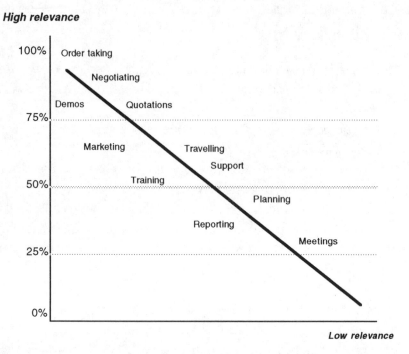

Figure 3.3   The relevance of a salesperson's activities

storage). They soon realised that the only activity for which the customer would be willing to pay, and therefore the only activity relevant to customer needs, was processing. Thus if they could eliminate the other (irrelevant) elements of cycle time, they could reduce the cost and increase the speed of the manufacturing operation.

A sample of the 30 activities within the assembly shop is set out in Figure 3.4. This table shows how GE classified these activities as value-adding (relevant to the customer); grey (partially relevant); and waste (irrelevant to the customer), and how many people were involved in each one of them. Managers were surprised to find that irrelevant activities engaged half the workforce – an unrivalled opportunity for time, and therefore cost, reduction.

To eliminate this non-value-adding work, managers needed to understand its causes. Through discussion, observation and examination of time records, managers classified the causes in three ways – those

ACTIVITIES	PEOPLE	VALUE-ADDING	GREY	WASTE
Assemble	11	11		
Accumulate material	4			4
Expedite material	2			2
Wait for material	1			1
Others	14		5	9
TOTAL	32	11	5	16
	100%	34%	16%	50%

Figure 3.4   Activity analysis of the GE assembly shop

within their control (for example, problems with stocking procedures); those arising outside their control (for example, problems caused by the frequent issue of engineering change notices); and problems of a long-term nature (for example, those relating to the number of parts needed to make the product). As managers studied the classifications, two major causes became evident: the poor flow of materials, and the receipt of defective parts from suppliers. As a result, they took three specific actions: they revised the plant layout to reduce the movement and accumulation of material; they introduced new material handling equipment; and they allowed hourly paid personnel to contact suppliers directly concerning quality issues.

After nine months of redesigning the assembly process, the results of continuously eliminating the irrelevant activities were dramatic. Total payroll costs were reduced by 21 per cent; the time taken to convert the raw material into the finished product fell by as much as 60 per cent; defects at the final test stage fell by 50 per cent; and work in progress reduced by 55 per cent.

The question as to whether work adds value can be seen in two stages. So far only the first stage has been considered – whether the work is relevant. The second question concerns how well the activity is performed – or, phrased differently, whether the work is of good quality.

A piece of work can be defined as being of good quality if it is carried out correctly the first time. Failure to perform good quality work results in correction, rework, chasing and rescheduling. None of these activities adds any value for customers. Given a choice, customers will not pay for these inefficiencies. Moreover, poor quality work wastes time and leads to extended problems throughout the chain. For example, failure to complete a sales order correctly can cause extra work for production, order processing, sales, shipment, accounting and debt collection. Moreover, self-preservation attitudes and functionally based performance measures guarantee that the problem is passed on to the next team.

The paradox in this analysis is that the highest quality work is often that which corrects problems caused earlier in the particular process. Thus one of the key issues facing systems designers is how to record the causes of poor quality work to ensure that the offending process team is properly identified and charged with the extra costs they cause. For example, a salesperson might be prevented from spending all his or her time selling (a value-adding activity) because of the inefficiency of factory deliveries. So the time spent by the salesperson correcting the problem should be charged to the production process. Determining those responsible for poor quality work is not always easy. But in practice patterns are likely to emerge. For instance, if more than one salesperson continually reports the same reasons for wasted time, it is likely that managers will be clearer as to why problems are caused.

While relevance of work has been a standard part of activity analysis for some time, the analysis of activity costs by quality of work is less common. The following example illustrates how the two aspects of non-value-adding costs can be reconciled.

The president of Process Plus, a US chemical firm, having performed an activity analysis, discovered that 70 per cent of the time of researchers was spent in meetings, 20 per cent on safety and disposal activities, 5 per cent on miscellaneous activities, and only 5 per cent on actual research. But further investigation revealed that within the 5 per cent of value-adding time, there were many delays and much rework. For example, 90 per cent of experiments were rescheduled because of equipment problems and, of the experiments that were conducted, 38 per cent had been done previously. But no one knew because the library records were out of date.

The study first examined whether work was relevant, and discovered that only 5 per cent of work fell into this category. But a deeper investigation pursued a different line of enquiry: was the relevant work of good quality? It was found that much of the 'relevant' work failed to meet this test. Thus the two-step procedure of analysing work by its relevance and quality finally identified that only a small proportion of work truly added value for the customer. It is this type of analysis that forms the basis of the horizontal information system which we explain later in this chapter.

Why is the analysis of work by relevance and quality important? The most obvious reply is that it guides managers towards the right problem-solving approach. To deal with questions of irrelevance managers must reorganise work flow in such a way as to minimise this unnecessary (and costly) work by, for example, encouraging salespeople to spend more time selling and less time reporting. Questions of poor quality demand a different approach. By identifying the sources of problems, the offending person, or team, can be held to account for their actions, and thus learn from their mistakes.

Failure to achieve high levels of relevant and quality work within the value chain has destructive effects on the speed of processes. The analogy with a leaking water pipe might help to explain the effects. Water enters the pipe in full flow, but soon the cracks, bottlenecks and leaks cause the speed of flow to turn to a trickle as water moves along the pipe (see Figure 3.5).

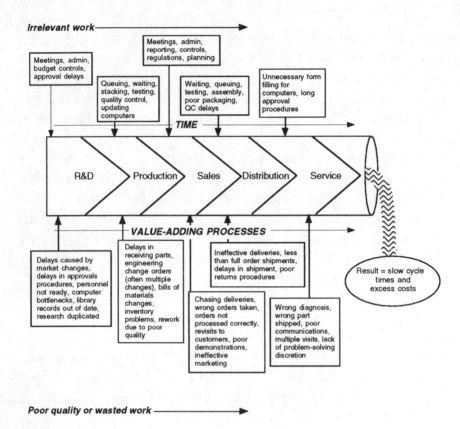

Figure 3.5   The leaking value-adding process

ATTEMPTS TO ELIMINATE
NON-VALUE-ADDING WORK

If the actual level of value-adding work in a firm is, say, 20 per cent, then improving work flows and reducing waste might easily improve this proportion to 30–40 per cent, thus effecting a huge reduction in costs. Performing the same operation in half the time not only saves money but provides new opportunities.

Various approaches have been tried over recent years to eliminate non-value-adding work, including quality programmes, 'workout' programmes, work audits, process mapping, business process reengineering, and activity-based management. Of these, the last two have received most exposure.

Reengineering

Hammer and Champy see reengineering as 'starting over', or taking a blank sheet of paper and redesigning the business from scratch while using none of the previous structures, departments or styles. There are many successful reengineering stories. Hammer and Champy cite those at Hallmark, Taco Bell, Capital Holding and Bell Atlantic as programmes which have brought major improvements in profitability – but it takes courage to withstand the attendant dislocation and backlash.

To illustrate the power of reengineering in eliminating non-value-adding costs, Hammer recounts what happened when Ford compared its accounts payable procedures with those at Mazda. In the 1980s Ford's North American accounts payable department employed over 500 people. Managers, in their efforts to reduce costs, targeted reductions of 20 per cent, which in the light of other restructuring programmes seemed acceptable – until they looked at the same operation at Mazda, which employed just four people. Ford's reaction was to revise dramatically its targets, but to do this required a reevaluation of the work involved in the accounts payable process.

When Ford managers analysed their existing systems they realised the full extent of the problem. Documents were moved around for checking and approval at a rapid rate, and many employees spent their time matching orders to goods received notes, and matching goods received notes to purchase invoices. In fact, 14 documentation checks were involved, which in turn entailed a high percentage of mismatches, reconciliation problems, letters and telephone calls, and generally resulted in slow approval procedures, unpredictable payment schedules and unhappy suppliers.

Ford managers decided to reengineer the process. Their first conclusion would have most accountants shaking their heads in disbelief – they dispensed with the need for purchase invoices. Now when a purchase order is issued it is simply recorded in an on-line database. When the goods arrive the goods received note is matched against this database record; if it is in order the goods are accepted and an automatic (electronic) payment generated; if it is incorrect the goods are rejected and returned to the supplier. At a stroke, Ford managers eliminated the need for checking, reconciling, chasing, matching, posting and summarising, which caused most of the work done previously. And of course costs plummeted.

By rethinking the entire process, and designing new information processing systems to meet its requirements, Ford achieved a 75 per cent reduction in headcount (through eliminating unnecessary work), and had more efficient and satisfied suppliers (who were automatically paid if their first-time deliveries were correct), as well as more satisfied auditors (who only had to check four entries).

This example is not untypical of the effects of reengineering, although more recent studies have suggested that its impact on jobs is not usually so dramatic. But reengineering is, by definition, project based and likely to lead only to a 'once and for all' change. Attempts to measure subsequent performance are rare.

Activity-based management

A number of companies have used activity-based management (ABM) as a starting point for eliminating non-value-adding work and, more generally, for improving the way processes are managed. The following two cases illustrate the power of ABM.

In 1992, Hewlett-Packard conducted a survey into the effectiveness of one of its UK sales regions. It was made clear at the outset that the purpose of the project was not to cut costs, but to identify bottlenecks which were causing problems for customers and potentially damaging sales. The company was enjoying a good year – sales had increased by 20 per cent and costs were within budget. However, there was a feeling among salespeople that performance could be even better.

Managers were asked to consider the necessity of the tasks they performed and the value that these tasks contributed to the overall selling process. Because little hard data was available on the nature of the work performed, considerable reliance was placed on the detailed knowledge of employees. The work of the sales region was analysed into six key processes, and each process was further broken down into its constituent activities.

The percentage of non-value-adding work for each process is shown in Figure 3.6. The study also produced a hit list of problems to be attacked. Figure 3.7 shows the percentage of waste in ten detailed activities.

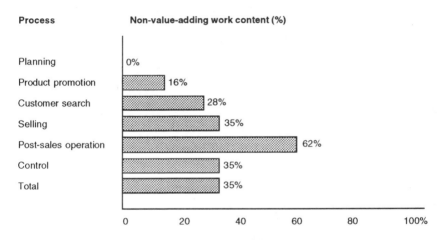

Figure 3.6   Percentage of non-value-adding work

These figures clearly demonstrate the extent of the problem. For example, less than a quarter of deliveries were correctly dealt with first time, and only half of the sales orders were correctly processed. For the sales region as a whole, 35 pence in every pound was spent on wasted work – a huge opportunity for profit improvement. Armed with this type of information, HP managers implemented measures to reduce these unnecessary costs. By March 1994 more than half the non-value-adding costs had been 'recovered' by better negotiating skills, more effective communication and less wasted time.

Problem/*Activity*	Non-Value-Adding %
Incorrect *deliveries*	76
Ineffective *negotiations*	31
Poor *order processing*	45
Incorrect *quotations*	43
Inconsequential *demonstrations*	66
Incorrect *configurations*	53
Ineffective *relationship building*	42
Wasted *time with partners*	41
Wasted *travelling time*	24
Ineffective *communications*	39

Figure 3.7   Percentage of waste

These cost reductions have made a significant contribution to improved profits at HP over the past few years (with the UK as the star performer). The managing director of HP in the UK, John Golding, said on the announcement of the results, 'the company's performance was the result of quality programmes, eliminating waste, consolidating operations, and keeping expenses under control.'

The second study concerns a retail operation with 55 branches. After an investigation showed that the major reason for declining market share was poor service, largely owing to the unavailability of stock, attention was focused on the accounting department as the provider of data to the stores on stock availability. The accounting department had three main purposes – to process invoices for payment; to manage inventory; and to prepare journal entries – and it also performed a number of less important 'other' activities. To see how its service could be improved, these processes were broken down into their component activities. For example, invoice processing entailed the cumulative and sequential activities of receiving, processing, entering and paying the invoices.

Figure 3.8 shows the activity centres; the detailed activities; the basic functions of these activities; the percentage of time spent directly on these basic functions (the time spent on good quality work); the total amount spent on each function; and the value of quality work.

Item	Activity	Basic Function	% Value Added	Cost ($/yr)	Value Added ($/yr)
	Receive	Separate invoices	30	67,725	20,318
INVOICE	Process	Code invoices	50	201,600	100,800
PROCESSING	Enter	Enter invoices	60	335,425	201,255
	Payment	Prepare cheque	30	67,250	20,175
	Monitor	Check			
INVENTORY		transactions	5	189,440	9,472
MANAGEM'T	Balance	Make corrections	10	322,560	32,256
	Expense	Record entry	10	113,066	11,307
JOURNAL	Inventories	Record entry	10	113,066	11,307
ENTRIES	Liabilities	Record entry	10	113,066	11,307
	Expense allocation	Assign cost	15	19,200	2,880
	Variance analysis	Calculate difference	50	21,504	10,752
OTHER	Reporting	Lost items	25	21,658	5,415
	Cash reqs	Cumulative reqs	50	14,438	7,219
	TOTALS			1,600,000	464,948

Figure 3.8   Activity analysis of the accounting department

Of the total cost of running the department ($1,600,000), only $464,948 was spent on value-adding activities – less than 30 cents in every dollar. By understanding the causes of the problems managers set out systematically to eliminate them. In all they were able to identify actions which took out up to 80 per cent, or approximately $900,000, of the wasted work. Specifically, they:

❑ reduced the number of suppliers of raw materials by 50 per cent. This reduced greatly the need to receive, process and enter (often incorrect) invoices

❑ implemented new, automated electronic data interchange systems to allow faster exchange of data between locations

❑ identified other major areas of improvement by better verification of source data, thereby eliminating the need for many of the corrections

Most importantly, the activity analysis allowed the department to improve the quality of its service to its users. Thus suppliers were paid more quickly, store managers received more up-to-date information on inventory levels, and customers ceased to be frustrated by poor availability of products. The results of these investigations led to a clearer understanding that only an analysis of *work* provides the real clues to cost savings and improvements in efficiency and service.

FAILING TO SOLVE THE PROBLEMS

Significant progress has been made in recent years in the fight to eliminate non-value-adding work. In both the Hewlett-Packard and retail company studies, for example, noticeable changes were seen in the attitudes of managers and workers. They started to work as a team with the common purpose of satisfying customer needs. This change did not occur through attending seminars or heeding management exhortations, but through the development of trust and understanding reinforced by the new information. By working together and sharing information they began to make the sort of fundamental changes that they would otherwise scarcely have believed possible.

Total quality management, reengineering and activity-based management have all attacked the problem of non-value-adding work in different ways and all can claim success stories, but the record is more one of spasmodic breakthroughs than sustained success. These successes are invariably project based, where teams of managers have identified and tackled particular trouble spots. Often they have been driven by external consultants who leave a vacuum of sponsorship and support when the job has been finished.

Player and Keys have identified a number of reasons why ABM projects fail. These include a lack of management commitment; failure to set clear objectives; and poor links between ABM programmes and other management initiatives such as just-in-time, total quality and reengineering. But it is the lack of employee involvement which is perhaps the common thread. As the authors acknowledge:

> Employees must be involved in creating, implementing, and continuously improving the ABM system...improvement should be normal rather than exceptional.

At best activity-based management offers managers signposts to problems which can then be dealt with on an *ad hoc*, project-by-project basis. What it doesn't do is provide a structured measurement approach to the depth and nature of these problems and thus cannot help managers prioritise their limited resources. To capture the benefits of this type of analysis *systematically* requires a new approach, one based on a horizontal information system.

HORIZONTAL INFORMATION SYSTEMS PROVIDE THE REAL NUMBERS

Horizontal systems show managers how costs are caused by analysing the quality and relevance of work. In a horizontal system, the *time* of individual workers, or groups of workers, is recognised to be the cause of activity costs, whereas an ABM system usually starts from the *costs* of activities.

At the heart of a horizontal information system lies a new measurement index – an index of *value-adding work* (see Figure 3.9). Such an index distinguishes, at its core, between work which is irrelevant to the needs of the customer (the relevance criterion) and work which is performed badly and necessitates correction (the quality criterion). It provides an activity framework within which teams and workers can measure the value of their work and record any significant periods when they are engaged on work of no value.

But how does an organisation, or business unit, employing large numbers of people begin to derive this sort of detail? Activity analysis again points the way. Most employees are involved in only a small

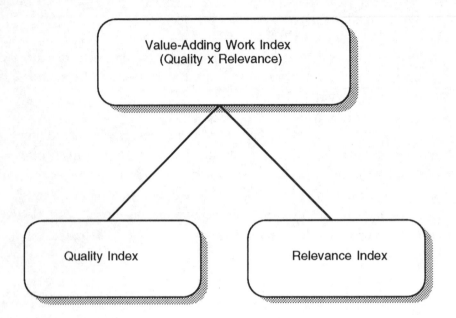

Figure 3.9   Value-adding work index

number of major activities. By borrowing a well-worn management
concept – *exception reporting* – a horizontal information system can
record when a person spends time working on their non-core activities.
In other words, *by recording what people are not supposed to be doing*
(correcting work caused by others, revisiting customers, chasing, changing and generally solving problems), a picture can be painted by the
information system of those costs that add no value to the customer.

The basic concepts of horizontal systems

Each system designer will have their own approach to the way a horizontal system might handle data and report results. What is described
here is just one possible approach. It starts with an 'activity ledger' (AL)
which runs parallel to the general ledger (GL). The AL contains a chart
of accounts comprising activity headings such as selling, travelling and
attending meetings. The GL and AL use the same cost database – the
difference lies in the analysis.

The strength of such a system depends on its ability to analyse work into its value-adding and non-value-adding components. We will use the example of Fred, a salesman with Company A, to illustrate how this might be done. There are four stages.

Stage 1: Translating general ledger costs to activity ledger costs
The activity ledger has been constructed and loaded onto Company A's computer system. Fred works within the order-generation process team. He is involved in only four 'standard' activities and the time he is assumed to spend on each one is recorded in his personal file. His activities and time spent are as follows: selling (40 per cent); travelling (20 per cent); reporting (20 per cent); and attending meetings (20 per cent). Whether Fred actually spends his time in exactly this way is unimportant at this stage in the analysis.

Fred's total costs for the month are $5000 and are shown in Figure 3.10. These costs not only include Fred's direct costs (salary, benefits and travel), but also any other costs he incurs (e.g. the cost of his telephone calls). These costs are shown in Figure 3.10 in both the traditional GL and the AL format.

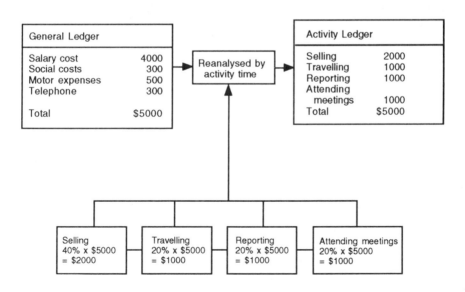

Figure 3.10   Fred's activity costs within a horizontal system

Stage 2: Determining the costs of irrelevant work

Stage 2 considers whether Fred's activities are relevant to the customer. The question of relevance is applicable only to individual activities and thus can be set (and reset) by managers. Such 'reviews' might take place, say, every six months. Employees have personal files within the system which tells the computer who they are, where they work, which 'accounting costs' they use and in what proportion, and to which standard activities their time is allocated. These relationships can of course be changed at any time. Thus relevance ratings are already known to the computer system and can be applied automatically to Fred's activity costs. In his case these relevance ratings are: selling (100 per cent); travelling (75 per cent); reporting (50 per cent); and attending meetings (25 per cent).

At the end of Stage 2 Fred's activity costs have been analysed into those which provide value for the customer (i.e. relevant work) of $3500 and those providing no value (irrelevant work) of $1500. Figure 3.11 shows how they might appear within the horizontal system. Up to this point Fred has provided no data concerning how well his work was performed. The computer has simply used its predetermined ratios and relevance factors to re-analyse Fred's costs. It is only at Stage 3 that Fred might cause the system to react to any 'exceptional' time which has been spent on poor quality work.

Activity Ledger		Relevance rating	Cost of irrelevance	Value-adding cost
Selling	2000	100%		2000
Travelling	1000	75%	250	750
Reporting	1000	50%	500	500
Attending meetings	1000	25%	750	250
TOTALS	$5000		1500	3500

Figure 3.11   Fred's activity costs showing the cost of irrelevant activities

Stage 3: Determining the costs of poor quality work

The computer system will assume that Fred's time has been spent on good quality work *unless instructed otherwise*. This is an important point and goes to the heart of the horizontal system. Fred will only tell the system *by exception* if time is not spent on normal activities. By concentrating on this exceptional time and identifying its causes, the system can begin to build a picture of why work does not add value.

Let's assume that Fred's work was in fact subject to a number of distractions, and that he had to spend a considerable amount of time chasing the factory to ensure that deliveries were completed, and revisiting existing customers who were unhappy with aspects of post-sales service. Fred has reported that 60 per cent of his selling time was taken up with this unnecessary work. Thus the value-adding content of his selling activity is reduced from $2000 to $800 (i.e. by reducing his value-adding cost by 60%).

The final picture of Fred's costs within the horizontal system can now be seen. Figure 3.12 sets out the full report and analysis of Fred's value-adding work, showing his final value-adding work index (VAWI) to be 46 per cent. The three indices are shown in their positive form. The quality index measures good quality work (76 per cent); the relevance index measures relevant work (70 per cent); and the value-adding work index measures the net amount of Fred's work (and cost) which adds value for the customer (46 per cent).

FRED'S VA WORK INDEX	Activity Cost	NVA Costs (Poor Quality)	NVA Costs (Relevance)	Net VA Work	Quality Index	Relevance Index	VAWI
Selling	2000	1200	0	800	40.0%	100%	40.0%
Travelling	1000	0	250	750	100.0%	75%	75.0%
Reporting	1000	0	500	500	100.0%	50%	50.0%
Attending meetings	1000	0	750	250	100.0%	25%	25.0%
TOTALS	5000	1200	1500	2300	76.0%	70%	46.0%

Figure 3.12   Fred's value-adding work index

This report enables managers to see where and how improvements can be made. In other words, depending on priorities and resources, the report might trigger the type of investigation which occurred in both the HP and retail company cases. But the important aspect to stress is that this improvement is now measurable. Of course, the success of the system depends on Fred's understanding and support. This support might be more forthcoming if managerial action is taken to correct the causes of Fred's problems, for example by penalising the factory for poor deliveries and the service personnel for poor service.

Stage 4: Applying costs to products and customers
The final stage traces Fred's costs to products and customers. Although in practice this will involve the choice and use of 'cost drivers', it will be assumed here that Fred spends his time with only one customer (Customer Z). Is the total cost of $5000 to be charged to this customer? This is an important question, because the answer helps in large measure to determine the real profitability of Customer Z and thus whether or not this business is worthwhile.

First, there is little doubt that the value-adding cost of $2300 should be charged to the customer, as this represents relevant and good quality work. However, there is some doubt as to whether to charge the customer with the $1500 cost of irrelevant work. The best way perhaps is to show this cost separately on the customer profit statement. This has the powerful effect of telling managers that they must reorganise the way they do business with Customer Z to allow Fred to spend more of his time with the customer.

The next step concerns the treatment of the cost of poor quality work performed by Fred's colleagues, amounting to $1200. This cost should be handled internally between process teams, and there seems to be no reason to charge it to the customer. The only circumstance in which this might happen is when the work which caused the cost can be attributed directly to the customer (for example, if orders are wrongly submitted or extra levels of technical support demanded which entail multiple visits).

Finally, consider how Customer Z's profit and loss account might appear under the horizontal system. Assume that Customer Z's gross profit before Fred's costs amounts to $4000. Figure 3.13 compares the horizontal view of this profit with the traditional view. Under the horizontal system Customer Z's real profitability is much clearer and managers can see what action needs to be taken to improve it, whereas under the traditional view they are simply told that Customer Z is unprofitable, thus casting doubt on the relationship in the future.

Traditional system		Horizontal system	
Gross profit	4000	Gross profit	4000
Less: Selling costs	5000	Less: Value-adding costs	2300
Loss	($1000)	Real profit	1700
		Less: Costs of irrelevant work	1500
		Profit before quality costs	200
		Less: Costs of poor quality	
		work	1200
		Accounting loss	($1000)

Figure 3.13   Comparison of traditional and horizontal profits for Customer Z

Some of the practical issues involved in designing and implementing horizontal systems will be discussed in more detail in Chapter 8.

The case for horizontal systems rests on the following attributes:

❑ *They provide a structured approach to measuring value-adding performance.* By reporting the proportion of work which adds value for customers and by identifying the causes of major non-value-adding problems, managers are in a position to monitor performance on a regular basis.

❑ *They emphasise the continuous improvement of business processes.* The value-adding work index places the quality and relevance of work right at the heart of the company. To see the value-adding work index improve step by step is to see the quality and relevance of work improve.

❑ *They provide an open information framework that binds managers and workers together in a common purpose.* By providing performance indices at team level and making teams responsible for their own performance, a horizontal system links performance to customer value, not to the more narrow interests of executives and shareholders.

❑ *They link the causes of costs with their effects.* By providing each worker and each team with a clear set of value-adding activities, workers and managers can immediately recognise whether work or its associated costs either conforms to those activities or detracts from them.

❑ *They can be reconciled to the financial system and thus provide 'horizontal views' of information.* Horizontal systems provide alternative views of profitability by attributing activity costs to those product groups, customers, and markets which use them.

4

DEVELOP A HORIZONTAL
TEAM-BASED ORGANISATION

Achieving competitive success through people involves fundamentally altering how we think about the workforce and the employment relationship. It means achieving success by working with people, not by replacing them or limiting the scope of their activities. It entails seeing the workforce as a source of competitive advantage, not just as a cost to be minimised or avoided.

Jeffrey Pfeffer

AT THE HEART OF ANY SUCCESSFUL LONG-TERM STRATEGY LIES THE retention of satisfied profitable customers. But unless managers direct the actions, behaviour and rewards of the *workforce* towards satisfying customer needs, all the strategic planning in the world will be to no avail. Most organisations, however, are neither structured nor managed in a way which allows this to happen.

Traditional organisations typically have a hierarchical management structure. Managers 'manage' and workers are told what to do. The relationship between the two is frequently confrontational. Each group has a different agenda: managers represent the interests of shareholders (to maximise profits), and workers represent interests of their own (to maximise wages). But it is difficult to imagine a structure less designed to further the interests of the only person who pays the bills – the customer. And it is hard to imagine a structure less suited to *everyone's* ultimate objective – long-term growth and prosperity. There is simply no language within traditional structures and systems which talks about the delivery of customer value.

But there is a radically different view as to the role of the workforce in a successful organisation. Jeffrey Pfeffer, for example, offers powerful evidence that those companies which have made long-term commitments to their workforce, and placed them at the centre of their strategy, have been highly successful (as measured by financial criteria) over the long term. For example, he notes that the five top performing American companies by stock market growth over a 20 year period from 1972–92 are (in order): Southwest Airlines, Wal-Mart, Tyson Foods, Circuit City and Plenum Publishing. He further notes that none of these companies has any distinctive 'competitive advantage' such as product differentiation, economies of scale, high-technology products or protective patents. The only common thread is in their similar treatment of the workforce. Each company stresses long-term employment, high wages, high skill levels, participation and information sharing. They all exhibit high productivity, high quality, good service, and they reward value-adding performance. In his view the strength and commitment of the workforce constitutes their differentiator – their real source of competitive success.

Of course, not all firms would readily admit to adopting a confrontational regime. And, following the recent tidal wave of restructuring and reengineering, action to combat the worst effects of these approaches has, in many cases, already taken place. But has such action brought about the changes that Pfeffer espouses? Xerox's CEO, Paul Allaire, explains what is involved in making such changes:

> When most companies reorganise, usually they focus on the formal structure of the organisation – the boxes on the organisational chart... Typically, top management just moves people around or tries to shake up the company by breaking up entrenched power bases. Rarely do senior executives contemplate changing the basic processes and behaviours by

which a company operates. Until recently, Xerox was no different. In the 1980s, we went through a number of reorganisations. But none of them got at the fundamental question of how we run the company... The change we are making now is more profound than anything we've done before. We have embarked on a process to change completely the way we manage the company. Changing the structure of the organisation is only a part of that. We are also changing the processes by which we manage, the reward systems and other mechanisms that shape those processes, and the kind of people we place in key managerial positions. Finally, we are trying to change our informal culture – the way we do things, the behaviours that drive the business.

Changing management structures and styles in this way is no easy task. It is tantamount to changing the way the company is organised and how work is done. Businesses need to be remodelled into teams based around key processes, with each one providing value to specified customers. Each employee must have a clear view of the importance of his or her work. As Johnson has said:

Bottom-up empowerment, in my view, occurs when someone can say 'I know how my work, and the work of those who depend on me really combine to make a difference for our ultimate customers.'

Such an approach also depends for its success on the right information. We argued in the previous chapter that horizontal information systems offer a better way forward. By providing all workers with a 'template' of their standard activities, and 'rating' these activities according to their perceived value, horizontal systems can measure the value of work in any given period and by any given group. Moreover, by providing workers with the means to record any time spent on work which falls outside these standard parameters, non-value-adding work (and its causes) can also be tracked and measured.

The success of such a system depends entirely on employee support. This will be difficult to obtain unless workers can be convinced that the purpose of such systems is not to control what they do or how they spend their time. Rather it is to help teams to improve planning and to pinpoint problems. A relationship of trust and information sharing must exist. Indeed, Senge has argued that trust and openness are impossible to foster without shared information. In his view:

> People working together with integrity, authenticity and collective intelligence are profoundly more effective as a business than people living together based on politics, game-playing and self-interest.

But to reach this promised land, changes are needed in management structures, management styles, and reward and recognition systems.

FROM THE VERTICAL TO THE HORIZONTAL MODEL

Traditional vertical organisations are well understood. They typically divide work into functions and departments, and then into jobs and tasks. Managers are at the top of the chain of command. Their role is to match the right people with the right tasks, and then to measure, control and reward their performance. When problems arise, managers look to correct any design flaws in the system. These might include:

❑ whether to organise by product, division, area or market
❑ which functions to centralise or decentralise
❑ how to integrate across functional boundaries
❑ how to balance the roles of line and staff personnel
❑ how to determine the appropriate spans of control
❑ how to align individual and managerial roles and responsibilities with organisational performance measures
❑ how to plan, budget, and review performance

Vertical structures stress the importance of functional excellence, but invariably suffer from a lack of coordination between functions, departments, jobs and tasks.

The horizontal model looks at the organisation of work from a different perspective – that of the *customer*. It is characterised by a small number of core business processes, for example new product development (from concept to launch); production (from procurement to shipment); order generation (from marketing to payment); and customer service (from complaint to resolution), managed by 'cross-functional teams'. Speed of work is frequently cited as a particular advantage of process team formation. A particular feature of teams is that they have 'ownership' of their performance targets. The horizontal team-based model is illustrated in Figure 4.1.

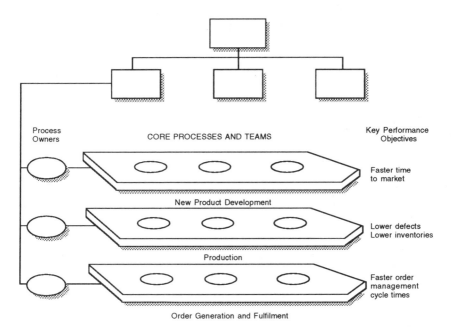

Process Owners

CORE PROCESSES AND TEAMS

Key Performance Objectives

Faster time to market

New Product Development

Lower defects
Lower inventories

Production

Faster order management cycle times

Order Generation and Fulfilment

Figure 4.1 Horizontal team-based structure

Consider how vertical and horizontal structures handle the purchasing of goods. In the traditional structure, four separate departments deal with the purchasing process. The purchasing department orders the goods, the quality control department checks them on arrival, the inventory department enters them into stock, and the accounts payable department finally ties the documentation together and pays the supplier. Each department has its own procedures to follow and the scope for delays and errors is obvious. Moreover, no one department is responsible for the speedy and effective completion of the process. In a horizontal structure, however, each step of the cycle is sequential within one integrated process, with one team clearly responsible for completing the work as quickly as possible. Figure 4.2 shows these contrasting approaches.

Vertical structure – four departments

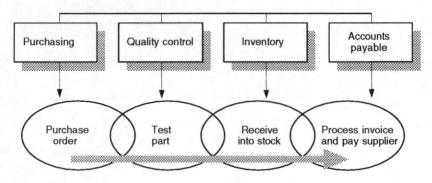

Horizontal structure – one integrated process

Figure 4.2   Comparison of a purchasing process

Motorola's government electronics group, GEG, produces hundreds of electronic products and systems for NASA, the US Defense Department and other government customers. Its managers believed that its supply organisation could be vastly improved by adopting a horizontal structure. Purchased materials accounted for more than half its total costs. Before redesign, GEG followed a functional, decentralised approach to supply management. A number of departments were duplicated both at group and divisional levels. In fact, seven levels of management separated the head of supply management from front-line employees. The objectives of the department were to purchase parts at the lowest cost and the highest quality, and the 700 staff were measured on a variety of individual tasks from purchasing to inspection. Although many workers possessed skills such as knowledge of the range of available parts, costs of redundant parts were high, coordination was poor, and relationships with suppliers were adversarial rather than mutually supportive. To combat these problems, GEG managers adopted a horizontal structure based on process teams.

Managers debated whether to centralise activities but realised that, although volume purchasing might improve, responsiveness to divisions might decline. So they decided to do something different – to design a supply management organisation as an end-to-end process that transforms the contributions of suppliers into the satisfaction of customers, both internal and external To achieve this they had not only to deliver on time and at the right price, but also focus on quality and the elimination of non-value-adding work. Previously the organisation had concentrated entirely on managing orders and price.

New performance measures were developed, including percentage of rejects, late deliveries, and cycle times. Front-line teams were charged with meeting performance targets based on these new criteria. The redesigned operation now resides only at group level, has fewer than 500 employees and just two levels between the head of supply management and the teams. The only remaining functional role is quality assurance, but quality management has been told to eliminate its inspection role and transfer it to the teams or to suppliers themselves. A recent McKinsey & Co report summarised the benefits to the division:

> In the two years since Motorola GEG's supply management organisation made the change, for example, deliveries and requisition cycles have fallen by a factor of four, supplier quality has increased by a factor of ten, and headcount has plunged by 30%. At the same time, there has been a dramatic growth in a wide variety of both individual and team-based skills. These results are not unique.

As noted earlier, adopting a horizontal structure does not simply mean flattening the management hierarchy and placing more people in front of customers, although this seems to be a common objective of many restructuring programmes. No matter how flat an organisation gets, no matter how many different functions interact directly with customers, customers want something else – they want their orders handled quickly, accurately and cost effectively. They don't want more people to talk to. This customer-based view was well explained in a recent article:

The order management cycle offers managers the opportunity to look at their company through a customer's eyes, to see and experience transactions the way customers do... In the course of the order management cycle (OMC), every time the order is handled, the customer is handled. Every time the order sits unattended, the customer sits unattended. Paradoxically, the best way to be customer-oriented is to go beyond the customer to the order; the moment of truth occurs at every step of the OMC, and every employee in the company who affects the OMC is the equivalent of a front-line worker... The best way for managers to learn this lesson is effectively to staple themselves to an order. They can then track an order as it moves through the OMC, always aware that the order is simply a surrogate for the customer... Here's what managers don't do: they don't travel horizontally through their own vertical organisation. They don't consider the order management cycle as the system that ties together the entire customer experience and that can provide true customer perspective.

Many writers now believe that customers themselves should be directly involved in the processes. They need, for example, to know at any time where their orders are in the system and who is dealing with the goods they have returned. They need to be connected to the supplier through on-line computer systems. And they need continuous information.

Vertical structures, with their internal focus, cannot easily generate this information, even if they are stretched, bent and overlaid with the immense power of modern computer systems. Nor can they easily identify, encourage and reward value-adding work. To realise the full power of the workforce, organisations must embrace the 'horizontal' model.

THE HORIZONTAL TEAM-BASED MODEL

Hammer and Champy have done much to popularise the process-based, or horizontal, organisation. This is their view of the future business structure:

In the post industrial age, companies will be founded and built around the idea of re-unifying the tasks which are currently fragmented by the command–control business structure. These tasks will be re-unified into coherent business processes... A process is a set of activities that, taken together, produce a result of value to a customer.

Most companies have between five and ten basic processes. The CEO of Allied Signal, Lawrence Bossidy, argues that:

every business has maybe six basic processes. We'll organise around them... The people who run them will be the leaders of the business.

Recent evidence has shown that process teams can deliver much higher levels of productivity than their functional counterparts. Womack and Jones, for example, argue:

By eliminating unnecessary steps, aligning all steps in an activity in a continuous flow, recombining labour into cross-functional teams dedicated to that activity, and continually striving for improvement, companies can develop, produce, and distribute products with half or less of the human effort, space, tools, time, and overall expense. They can also become vastly more flexible and responsive to customer desires.

But the main benefit of the team-based approach concerns the productivity of work. By reorganising around key processes and activities, attention is focused on how work is *performed*. As a general rule, the fewer the steps involved in a process, the more efficient is the process. Well-managed processes generally require fewer people to carry out activities. For example, they don't need the chasers, the inspectors, the problem solvers, the supervisors, the reconcilers, the counters, the movers, the stackers or the rework department. Perceptions of work are also changed – team members now work for customers (not for superiors) – and managers become 'coaches' rather than bosses.

Each company needs to design and develop a structure which is appropriate for its own particular business. Nevertheless, there are some guiding principles which can be followed in the design of a successful horizontal team-based organisation, which are explained in the following pages.

Flatten the hierarchy and minimise non-value-adding work

To flatten hierarchies, firms must recombine fragmented tasks, review each activity within each new process, and eliminate activities which add no value. As a general rule, the broader the work flow assigned to a process team, the more the scope for problem solving, innovation, and the elimination of unnecessary work. The very act of remapping functional tasks into core processes can highlight significant areas where (often huge) cost savings can be made. This happened at one of Hewlett-Packard's manufacturing plants in Scotland. Following an extensive review of performance, HP managers redesigned their business operations into six key processes. Figure 4.3 shows the result of this new design.

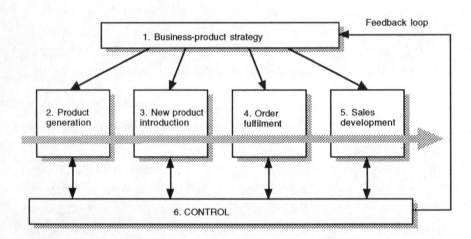

Figure 4.3   Manufacturing's six key processes at a Hewlett-Packard (UK) company

When managers re-analysed the old, functional costs into the new structure, they were surprised to find that 40 per cent of these costs did not easily fit the value-adding activities identified within each process (see Figure 4.4). The R&D and marketing departments were the biggest offenders. According to HP executive Jim Rigby:

> It came as no shock to find the manufacturing element of the order fulfilment process to be the most efficient. After all, production departments have a historic fixation for variance and standards deviation reporting. Also, they are usually the people who readily apply TQM to process improvements – unlike R&D, marketing, and administration who are too busy to improve. If only they knew.

PROCESS	MFG	R&D	MKTG	ADMIN	TOTAL	NVA%	NVA COSTS
Business-product strategy	20	500	320	100	940	30	282
Product generation	500	3,800	400	50	4,750	50	2,375
New product introduction	340	340	810	40	1530	40	612
Order fulfilment	2,520	10	30	240	2,800	15	420
Sales development	100	50	1,100	70	1,320	50	660
Control	800	200	300	690	1,990	40	796
TOTAL	4,280	4,900	2,960	1,190	13,330	40	5,145

Figure 4.4   Process cost analysis at HP (£000s)

Assign the 'ownership' of processes and process performance

Strong leadership is as important in a horizontal structure as in a vertical one. Indeed, in the early phase of the new team-based structure, tough demands are placed on team leaders. They must help the team set its performance objectives and be accountable for achieving them (a topic discussed in more depth in Chapter 5).

Ownership of processes, and responsibility for achieving targets, were major factors in Kodak's efforts to improve the performance of its film products business. This business was reorganised into six manufacturing 'streams', each supported by a range of technical expertise. One of the six was known as the 'Zebra team', comprising 1500 employees responsible for producing 7000 black and white film products. But the Zebra team leaders had a clear objective of restoring the image of black and white film and producing high quality products which 'delighted' customers. They dedicated themselves to building capability, improving teamwork, and spreading open communication throughout the flow of work, and made it clear that leaders were there to remove obstacles and delays and resolve any hand-off issues within the teams themselves.

Make teams the building blocks of the horizontal structure

It has been shown time and again that teams regularly produce outstanding performance largely because they bring a wider range of skills and experience to bear on the issues at hand. However, pulling together a number of specialists and giving them targets and objectives does not make them into an effective team. A well-designed team comprises a group with complementary skills who share a common purpose.

In recent years GE has slashed its management layers from 9 to 4, cut its head office staff from 2100 to under 1000, and adopted a team-based structure with between 15 and 25 staff to one team leader (this compared to the old functional management–staff ratio of 5 or 6). Several GE factories now claim to have only one level of management, and some claim to have none at all – just a collection of self-managing teams who make all their own decisions. Over this period of change GE's revenue has increased from $27 billion to $60 billion and its stock market value has soared.

Xerox has also changed to a team-based approach. One particularly interesting example of the company's change in thinking is in its utilisation of research and development expenditure. Under the old regime, business units would submit multiple applications for R&D resources and then negotiate as to which projects should receive funds. For example, by asking for $50 million a business unit manager would know in advance he or she would have a reasonable change of receiving $40 million, and so on. Now the process has been turned on its head. Unit managers have to explain what they expect to deliver and what resources they need. In effect, the spending priorities are now set by those closest to customers – that is, by the teams.

Team performance should be supported by functional expertise. Womack and Jones have suggested that functions such as marketing, finance, engineering and computing become 'centres of excellence'. In this model, employees' loyalties and career paths are geared to functions, but they spend time on secondment to process teams. Functions don't deal with suppliers and customers on a day-to-day basis, but their role is to help build better relationships across the whole value chain. This leaves functional specialists with more time to step back from the 'daily crisis' and ensure that standards are being improved and best practice observed (e.g. through benchmarking). They are also able to keep a watching brief over competitive issues as they affect the value chain. This revised model is shown in Figure 4.5.

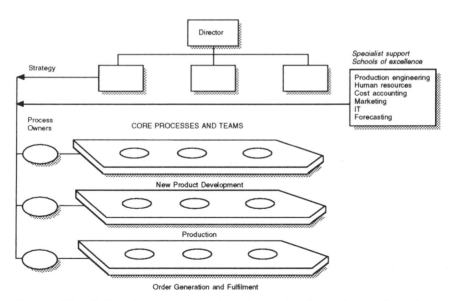

Figure 4.5   Role of support functions in the horizontal team-based structure

Develop self-managing teams

Vertical organisations tend to have a strict demarcation between managerial and non-managerial work. Indeed, this is the essence of the command and control structure. The people who know the reasons for poor performance – especially the causes of non-value-adding work – are neither encouraged nor rewarded for suggesting or making improvements. In the traditional structure this is the role of management. In self-managing teams this is no longer the case.

Milliken, an American textile manufacturer employing 14,000 people, won the Baldrige quality award in 1989. The company puts this success down to a continuous commitment to its workforce (termed 'associates'), organised in self-managing teams. For instance, any worker can stop the production line if a quality or safety problem is detected.

Teams at Motorola are responsible for setting their own objectives, scheduling, peer evaluation and job descriptions. Teams solve problems as they arise. Bottlenecks, delays or poor quality incoming parts are dealt with without interrupting the flow of work. Teams do the *real work* – they must also do the *real management*.

Encourage multiple competencies

Vertical structures are built around the specialisation and division of labour, but the advantages argued for specialisation are often illusory. As noted in Chapter 3, knowledge workers frequently spend little time creating and designing new products. The reality is that 'specialists' are so often embroiled in the maelstrom of day-to-day problem solving that their real expertise is rarely used.

In a team-based structure it is the diversity of team skills which is important. Moreover, it is the responsibility of each member to adapt to new challenges and requirements. Team members are often called on to perform different process-related activities and thus it is vital that they understand the whole process to which they contribute. At GE's

Salisbury plant, for example, every team member knows how to operate every machine in the plant (there are 70,000 product variations). They also understand the purpose of each machine and the impact on profitability of any downtime.

Provide teams with appropriate training and shared information

Experience has shown that people learn more effectively 'on the job' and that their motivation is heightened when such training is directly related to their ability to improve performance. The same goes for the provision of information. Most systems provide information either too late or too remotely for workers to use it to improve their performance. Best practice in horizontal structures is moving towards a training model based on a 'just in time – need to know' basis, which gives team members access to an on-line training service with technical expertise and immediate support.

Access to relevant on-line information can lead to improvements in performance. Teams at Kodak, for example, can gauge their performance immediately against measures of waste, quality, cost and efficiency, and are routinely trained in an understanding of which work adds value for the customer. Thus they can spot and deal with non-value-adding work as it arises. Workers are also trained in root cause analysis and statistical process control. One team charged with reducing wasted costs found a strong correlation between waste and machine utilisation rates, so they identified that the way to cut waste was to reduce the set-up time of machines.

Reward team-based, not individual, performance

Most workers are driven by factors other than money. Recognition, security, training and fair pay policies figure high on their lists. But it is difficult to argue with the view that the workforce should share in the fruits of their efforts. Conversely, if only executives and shareholders benefit from the results of a creative and skilled workforce, it is easy to understand how the seeds of discontent are sown. Clearly, the behaviour encouraged by incentive schemes is all important, and this relationship is discussed in more detail in the next chapter. There is, however, evidence that incentive schemes based on individual performance do not work. According to Alfie Kohn, reward systems can often be manipulated, people feel controlled, and the result is a rupturing of relationships within the firm:

> The surest way to destroy cooperation and, therefore, organisational excellence, is to force people to compete for rewards or recognition or to rank them against each other. For each person who wins, there are many others who carry with them the feeling of having lost, and the more these awards are publicised through the use of memos, newsletters, and award banquets, the more detrimental their impact can be.

Those incentive schemes that work best are those which emphasise team-based achievement and are clearly aligned with team targets. In GE's Bayamon, Puerto Rico, plant, for example, people are rewarded according to team-based targets and plant performance. But, as already argued, this kind of achievement is seldom measured by accounting systems. Deming claimed:

> The traditional financial mentality is the greatest impediment to quality management in the United States, because it deflects attention from the long-term interests of a company's operations and because traditional financial and accounting measures offer managers few of the insights they need to plan for the future.

THE CHANGING ROLE OF MANAGEMENT

James Champy has argued persuasively that failure to reform the practice of management may eventually undermine the very structure of reengineered companies. His belief is that the work of managers must change as much as that of workers. In particular, managers must reexamine their roles as teams become increasingly self-managed, and pay more attention to the provision of information, training and advice. In short, as workers take on more management tasks, managers must assume more leadership tasks. This is a difficult transition for managers who have often held the business together by acting as the 'organisational glue'.

And this is not all. Managers must also alter their *style* of management. Instead of issuing orders and micro-managing, they must become more effective at managing conflict and be better coaches. They can no longer assume that knowledge of the content of the job is the primary prerequisite for promotion. Openness and willingness to solve contradictory problems become more important in the process environment. Finally, Champy argues that managers must change management systems and, with fewer job descriptions and less hierarchy – compensation must be based more on skills and knowledge than on positions on organisation charts. If managers themselves cannot make the transition to the new structure, it may take 50 rather than 5 years to reverse the errors of the industrial revolution.

In some team-based organisations, team members are starting to earn higher salaries than their management colleagues. So why would anyone want to be a manager in such a structure? The answer was provided by an American executive when he noted that managers don't add much value supervising workers who are paid only $7 per hour. He said:

> Under the new work structures, managers have both more time and more responsibility for planning, preventing problems, learning about and implementing new technology, coaching and training employees in more effective practices, and most important, the strategic thinking that managers complain they never have time for.

Drucker has an analogous but equally penetrating view of the change in management's role under the new structure. He argues that:

There is a great deal of talk today about 'entitlement' and 'empowerment'. These terms express the demise of the command and control-
based organisation. But they are as much terms of power and terms of
rank as the old terms were. We should instead be talking about
responsibility and contribution. For power without responsibility is not
power at all; it is irresponsibility... What we should aim at is to make
people responsible. What we should ask is not 'What should you be
entitled to?' but 'What should you be responsible for?' The job of
management in the knowledge-based organisation is not to make
everybody a boss. The task is to make everyone a contributor.

Most employees have been trained in a functional discipline such as
engineering, accounting, computer programming or personnel. These
functions determine the job titles with which everyone is familiar.
However, it is only when individuals are brought together in cross-
functional teams that it becomes obvious that people from different
functions – even within the same organisation – often have a different
understanding of what constitutes strategy, of how performance is to be
defined and, indeed, what meaning is to be attributed to such 'simple'
words as cost or profit.

The problem is that team members inevitably bring to their new roles
the type of thinking which characterised their earlier functional job. The
friction caused by these different perceptions makes team-based success
more difficult to achieve. The team-based approach demands new thinking, a new understanding of responsibilities and authority, new (shared)
values and, most important of all, new measurement systems. According
to Meyer:

> At many companies that have moved from control-oriented, functional
> hierarchies to a faster and flatter team-based approach, traditional
> performance measurement systems not only fail to support the new
> teams but also undermine them. Indeed, traditional systems often
> heighten conflicts between multifunctional teams and functions that are
> vexing many organisations today.

SHARING A COMMON PURPOSE

The theories of Frederick Taylor were the foundation of mass production techniques in the early twentieth century. That employment policies should be designed to support the lowest unit cost of production continues to be influential in most western companies. But when comparing the performance of Japanese and American companies in the late 1980s Konosuke Matsushita, founder of Matsushita Electric, one of the largest and most successful companies in the world, argued:

> We will win and you will lose. You cannot do anything about it because your failure is an internal disease. Your companies are based on Taylor's principles. Worse, your heads are Taylorised, too. You firmly believe that sound management means executives on one side and workers on the other, on one side men who think and on the other side men who can only work. For you, management is the art of smoothly transferring the executives' ideas to the workers' hands... We have passed the Taylor stage... For us, management is the entire workforce's intellectual commitment at the services of the company.

Pfeffer has argued equally strongly that long-term success is based on a committed and skilled workforce. Indeed, this success can be mirrored to some extent at the national level. Those governments and companies that have pursued policies of high wages, high productivity, high quality and long-term employment appear to have been more successful than those that have followed policies designed to minimise costs through low wages, maximum labour flexibility, part-time and contract-based work and low levels of employee protection. It might be argued that Japan and Germany have pursued the former policies over the past 50 years, while the USA and Britain have followed the latter.

Britain, in particular, has suffered badly during this period from management–worker confrontation, particularly from within the old 'smokestack' industries. Recent manifestations have occurred with the coal and auto industries. Many of Britain's industrial 'heroes' were those who 'stood up to the unions' and eventually eradicated old unproductive ways of working. But where now are the British coal, auto and ship-building industries? By and large they don't exist, at least not under British ownership. Confrontation and the constant striving for the lowest unit cost of labour have proved to be a distinctly unsuccessful formula for long-term survival.

There is however another side to the story. Take, for example, what happened to the Dunlop tyre operations in the UK in the mid-1980s – it was rundown, its 3000-strong workforce demoralised, and its business in terminal decline. In 1985 the Dunlop Tyre Company was acquired by a Japanese company, Sumitomo Rubber Industries, and renamed SP Tyres Ltd. The Japanese managers were not surprised to find a hierarchical and autocratic management style. Contact between senior management and the shopfloor was limited, and the main communication was through union representatives. The declining state of the business meant that the only news the unions ever heard was about cutbacks and redundancies – indeed, what other reason was there to talk to them? The changes which followed the new ownership were dramatic.

By introducing job security, team working and profit sharing, the new management gradually built a climate of trust. People from different functional groups were brought together for the first time, shared each other's problems, and learned how to focus on the needs of the customer. The company introduced the Japanese *kaizen* approach to continuous improvement, with each team setting its own targets. After three years, a total quality programme was introduced which reinforced the cultural changes. The programme was also extended to suppliers. Each team assumed full responsibility for the quality of its work and for passing only 'good' products to the next team.

Despite the temptation to show quick short-term results, the company's plans were not affected by economic factors or by market fluctuations. This consistency and stability enabled managers to concentrate on their primary goals of long-term growth and performance improvement. After nine years, turnover per employee increased by 130 per cent; unit output per employee by 100 per cent; waste fell by 52 per cent and service returns by 55 per cent. In one product area, waste fell by as much as 70 per cent while quality improved significantly. According to SP Tyres chairman, Gerald Radford:

> After nine years of working together there has been such an effective merging of British and Japanese approaches that we are no longer conscious of the distinction... Visitors to our plants will not hear any company songs...what they will find is a motivated and responsible workforce keen to do better.

As many traditional companies begin to realise the extent of their problems and start to focus more on customer-oriented performance, they may well find that even this is not enough. Indeed, important though they are, neither 'customer focus', 'time to market' nor 'total quality' provide all the answers. They are, in fact, fast becoming simply the accepted standards necessary for survival. Meanwhile leading-edge companies are investing heavily in the knowledge and skills of their workforces, and transforming these investments into long-term profits.

Bain & Co have shown that employees who stay with an organisation for 10 years are likely to be three times as productive than when they began employment. Evidence from the Marriott hotel group also supports this thesis. As a result of a study in two divisions of the company, researchers found that a 10 per cent reduction in employee turnover would reduce customer non-repeats by 1 to 3 per cent and raise revenues by $50 million to $150 million. The researchers concluded that even with generous estimates for recruitment and training costs, and low estimates for the cost of lost customers, reducing employee turnover by 10 per cent yielded savings that were greater than the operating profits of the two divisions combined. The key to improving profitability is to look at the service from the customer's point of view – not from the 'most efficient' and 'lowest cost' standpoint.

Many firms are recognising that researchers, engineers, designers and software experts must be encouraged to share their knowledge and be rewarded for so doing. But in most organisations the reverse is more likely to be the case. Budgeting and reward systems act as a powerful counterforce by emphasising good housekeeping and cost control. The result is that ingenuity, creativity and innovation are stifled and dispersed in small islands of knowledge, which are jealously protected. In many traditional companies, knowledge is power – indeed it is often the only insurance policy available to workers against losing their job – and therefore such knowledge is carefully guarded.

Teams are the engines of change. They break the mould of confrontation and enable its members to focus on customer value rather than factional self-interest. The strength of teams lies in the trust between members and between team managers and executives. However, trust can be easily broken if information is seen as the preserve of senior managers and thus subject to manipulation. The openness of horizontal systems addresses this problem. Their primary performance index measures value-adding work. Indeed, such an index may well serve as the focus of future incentive programmes and thus reinforce the drive for continuous improvement.

5

ALIGN PERFORMANCE MEASURES
WITH STRATEGY

What you measure is what you get. Senior executives understand that their organisation's measurement system strongly affects the behaviour of managers and employees. Executives also understand that traditional financial accounting measures like return-on-investment and earnings per share can give misleading signals for continuous improvement and innovation – activities today's competitive environment demands.

Robert Kaplan and David Norton

THE VIEWS OF KAPLAN AND NORTON GO RIGHT TO THE HEART OF performance measurement. Pithy catchphrases such as 'measure what matters' and 'what gets measured gets done' are frequently quoted in the management literature, and they are no less important for that. They get the key message across.

But what is it that *matters* and what should *get done*? While financial results clearly matter to shareholders, it is the battle for the hearts and minds of customers that matters most in the fight for business survival. And what needs to be done is to exceed customers' expectations by profitably providing high-quality products and services. Because measurement systems drive behaviour at all levels in the firm, the choice of measures is crucial to success.

Recognition of these issues, aided by strong support from management academics and consultants, has led to the widespread use of 'non-financial' measures to supplement financial results. Some company executives have gone beyond the 'supplementary' stage. For example, Bob Galvin, Motorola's ex-CEO, believed that quality training was useless unless top managers gave quality more attention than they gave the quarterly results. He dramatised the point at operations review meetings by insisting that quality reports came first, not last, on the agenda, and then left before the financial results were discussed.

Measures of quality, customer and employee satisfaction, innovation, cycle times and organisational learning have all been championed in recent years. But this very advocacy of new measures has given finance managers a different problem. How do they know if the results of their improvement programmes, even when all the (non-financial) measures point in the right direction, actually lead to financial gains? Is faith enough? Or is there more they can do to reconcile the two streams of information? As Fisher has pointed out:

> Understanding the strengths, weaknesses, and trade-offs in non-financial systems requires development of an overall framework that explains these interrelationships. Much of the uncertainty that companies face in implementing non-financial systems will disappear once an accepted framework is developed. Certainly a major missing link is a tie-in between non-financial performance measures and financial performance.

While the introduction of non-financial measures might seem like a giant step for management-kind, is it the answer that organisations are really looking for? Or are the early success stories tantamount to picking low-hanging fruit? In other words, was 'horizontal' performance so dire to begin with that any measures of improvement were bound to look impressive? In traditional operations, the measurement system is entirely focused on results, not on how they are achieved. This point was made recently by Howard Barrett, a senior manager at Arthur Andersen:

Historically we have tended to keep looking at the scoreboard. But looking at the scoreboard doesn't actually improve your game.

Much more can be done in a process-based structure. By measuring and improving the relevance and quality of value-adding work within processes, it is also likely that results-based measures will improve. But the order is critical – by concentrating solely on results, processes might never improve. Johnson made exactly this point:

Companies should focus on goals that matter, not goals that count. What matters in business is to create fulfilling jobs and to survive by profitably satisfying customer wants...accounting goals direct attention to effects not causes. Survival requires astute management of root causes. In today's global economy that means optimising a system of stable processes... In other words, accounting systems focus attention on an end result but do not specify the means to achieve that end. To achieve the accounting targets mandated by top management, subordinates are left to manipulate processes in any way they think fit. The long term result is unstable processes, unhappy customers, and loss of jobs. I think that result describes most large American companies in the last 30 years.

ALIGNING MEASURES WITH STRATEGY

Performance measures and reward systems, above all else, determine behaviour and influence decisions. In many organisations important decisions are taken, and measures of performance implemented, with little reference to the strategic framework. It is easy to see how strategy and performance can be driven in different directions. Moreover, reward systems often reinforce this divergence, and actively encourage the realisation of short-term gains at the expense of longer-term benefits.

Consider the following data from a study of the printer industry. Based on assumptions of 20 per cent market growth, 12 per cent annual price decline and a five-year product life cycle, the study showed that if the printer company met its budgetary targets but was six months late to market with the new product, the cumulative profit decline (over a five-year life) would be 31.5 per cent. But if the company overran its cost budget by as much as 30 per cent but got to the market on time (the *critical success factor*), the decline in profitability would be minimal – only 2.3 per cent (see Figure 5.1). The study offered clear evidence of managers reacting to the wrong (cost-based) performance measures, in markets in which success is based not on cost reduction, but on the speed of new product introduction. The conclusion to the report suggested that:

> Many managers fail to understand the benefits of getting to market first. The same program managers who know to the penny what an engineer will cost, and what profits will be lost if cost targets are missed, cannot begin to quantify the losses associated with a six-month slip in the development process. They willingly slow down the development process to contain the project budget or to hit the cost targets.

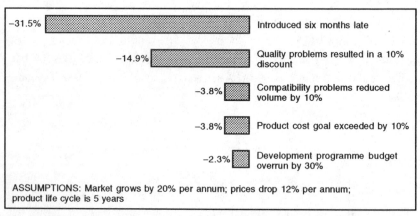

Figure 5.1   How product development problems affect profits (percentage decrease in cumulative profit)

Although financial measures *per se* rarely address the needs of internal decision makers, particularly in a process-based structure, there are a number of users for whom such measures remain important. This group includes analysts, shareholders, bankers, creditors and government departments, and those company executives who deal with them. These users should not be ignored. Indeed, whatever changes are made to performance measures, managers must understand that financial information (and the speed of its production) remains sacrosanct. Such measures include return on capital employed, profit before tax, earnings per share, and cash flow. There is nevertheless increasing recognition that financial performance can be improved by paying closer attention to measures which relate to strategic targets.

Each business unit, sales channel and distinct market warrants its own strategy and its own measurement systems. Many firms fall into the trap of having one measurement system for operational performance and a different one for rewards. For example, in young growing businesses the emphasis might be on longer-term goals, with incentive packages geared to market share, innovation and quality, whereas in more mature businesses the emphasis might be on short-term objectives such as maximising cash flow and earnings. One of the skills of top management must be to know when to change these targets and incentive plans.

One of the key strategic objectives at present is the speed of improvement of organisational learning. Indeed, many top executives believe that this is the new definition of competitive advantage. ADI chairman, Ray Stata, was one of the first to express the view that 'the rate at which individuals and organisations learn may become the only sustainable competitive advantage, especially in knowledge-intensive industries'. According to Zuboff:

> Learning is no longer a separate activity that occurs either before one enters the work-place or in remote classroom settings. Nor is it an activity preserved for a managerial group. The behaviors that define learning and the behaviors that define productivity are one and the same. Learning is not something that requires time out from being engaged in productive activity; learning is the heart of productive activity. To put it simply, learning is the new form of labor.

Which measures?

Even with a clearly defined strategy and a detailed list of critical success factors, it is not always easy to choose the right measures. Managers must ask what *behaviour* is to be influenced by the chosen measures. In other words, who should take notice of them? Shareholders, executives, managers, teams, employees? Nor is it the case that one measure can always be neatly related to one target. Targets often require multifaceted measures. With such a complex picture, what is needed is a 'balanced view', a matrix of measures that can show the performance of the organisation from the perspective of each of its stakeholders. The 'balanced scorecard' approach of Kaplan and Norton is one attempt to provide such a view.

Kaplan and Norton have suggested that the different performance measures should be linked to the organisation's overall vision and its strategic goals. Suppose that the primary objective is to become the number one supplier of goods and services to customers in total value delivered. How is this objective to be captured by the measurement system? The only measures of success which tell the external world how well this objective is being achieved are those used by the external world (shareholders, analysts, bankers etc.) to judge success. These measures are purely financial. Thus top managers are directly concerned with such a *financial* perspective, as determined by target measures of profitability (for example, return on sales, return on assets, and earnings per share) and measures of growth (for example, increase in sales).

To generate excellent financial results, organisations must have happy and profitable customers. To measure this aspect, the firm requires a *customer* perspective. So, for example, knowledge of the achievement of on-time delivery, excellent service and a better price–cost ratio require a different set of measures. Customers are satisfied because they like the quality and price of what is offered. High quality and low price in the long run come from excellent internal operations. Internal excellence depends on success in being fast to market, lowering manufacturing cycle time (indeed all cycle times) and producing few defects. Measures of continuous improvement for all these facets of internal operations are therefore required (an *internal* perspective).

Last but not least, Kaplan and Norton suggest a final perspective, which they term *organisational learning*. Thus to achieve their overall vision, organisations must generate a spirit of continuous learning, as measured by, for example, the rate of innovation and the percentage of the organisation's sales and profits which are derived from recently introduced products.

The four perspectives – financial, customer, internal and organisational learning – are mutually enforcing, but differ in nature. The measures which show the results of achieving internal excellence to the outside world are mainly but not exclusively financial, whereas those which address questions of innovation, operations and delivering value to customers are almost exclusively non-financial. Together they constitute the balanced scorecard (see Figure 5.2). 'Balanced' does not simply denote the relationship between financial and non-financial measures. It also refers to the different users. Thus the financial measures are more appropriate to shareholders, whereas employees and customers are more concerned with team-based and quality-based measures.

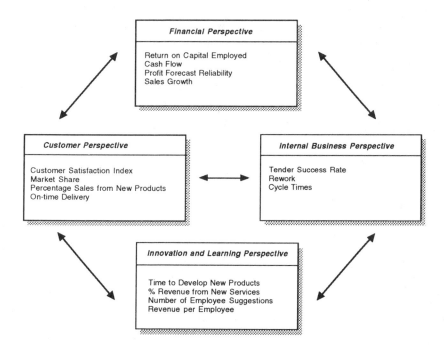

Figure 5.2   An example of a balanced scorecard

Rockwater, a worldwide leader in underwater engineering and construction, is one company which has enthusiastically adopted the balanced scorecard approach. The company first set down its mission: 'as our customers' preferred provider, we shall be the industry leader.' It then laid down five strategic objectives – services that surpass needs; customer satisfaction; continuous improvement; quality of employees; and shareholder expectations – and created a balanced scorecard to guide them towards these objectives.

The scorecard encompassed 20 measures, including the usual information on return on capital employed and cash flow, but also, more interestingly, measures for tender success rate, the amount of rework necessary, a safety indicator index, and a measure of hours spent with customers on new work.

The balanced scorecard has helped Rockwater establish a process view of operations, motivate employees and build stronger relationships with customers. A similar approach was adopted by Rank Xerox when it was shaken into action after discovering that, compared with its Japanese competitors, the defect rate within its manufacturing operations was ten times as high, its product lead times twice as long, and its unit cost equal to the Japanese selling price. It brought in new measures for customer and employee satisfaction, market share and return on assets. Rank Xerox's use of non-financial measures is now all embracing. According to Brendan Rogers, quality director:

> You ask if we spend too much time on these measures? Managers spend
> all their time on them. It's what they do.

On taking over at IBM, Lou Gerstner asked the heads of the 13 business units he established to sign contracts committing them to meet just seven performance measures. Four of them are the traditional financial yardsticks of revenue growth, profit, return on assets and cash flow. The other three are customer satisfaction, quality, and employee morale.

Scorecards are not confined to manufacturing organisations. Accountancy and consultancy firm Arthur Andersen preaches the new wave of performance measurement and has recently introduced five measures worldwide – recruitment, client acceptance, client satisfaction, market share and profitability. Each is subdivided into lower-level measures. For example, recruitment tracks the quality of its intake, the number of applications it receives, the number of interviews, the number of offers it makes, and the number of acceptances. Andersen believes that 'the quality of people we recruit is crucial, they are our raw product'.

Specific measures can be designed for specific purposes. Hewlett-Packard's former CEO John Young challenged employees to cut product development time in half over an eight-year period. The San Diego division was responsible for the development of new inkjet printers. Its managers took Young's request to heart and began by examining their past performance. Of the 12 previous projects they analysed, only two had been completed ahead of time and ten had slipped for various reasons – but this slippage had cost HP much in profitability.

Following the study, managers looked for a new measurement yardstick for use in new product development. They came up with 'break-even time' (BET), the period starting when a project begins and ending when profits from sales equal the cost of development and production. Unlike other measures, BET had the benefit of discriminating between products that were late but successful, and those that were on-time but a market failure. The results over the next few years were impressive. The new inkjet printers were developed in 22 months compared with four years previously. BET also helped elsewhere. For example, it helped one production line to cut manufacturing time from four weeks to just two days, and another department decreased order turnaround from six weeks to three days.

How should targets be set?

The balanced scorecard enables managers to focus on a limited range of important measures from different perspectives. But it is not always easy to set the right targets. For example, should last year's actual performance be the baseline? Or should the performance of competitors be used? And if so, how should detailed targets be set? Art Schneiderman of Analog Devices Inc (ADI) clearly stated the problem:

The basic flaw in current goal setting is that specific goals should be set based on knowledge of the means that will be used to achieve them. Yet the means are rarely known at the times the goals are set. The usual result is that if the goal is too low, we will underachieve relative to our potential. If the goal is too high, we will underperform relative to others' expectations. What's really needed to set rational goals is a means of predicting what is achievable if some sort of standard means of improvement were used.

ADI produces integrated circuits for the high-end data acquisition market. The company had consistently achieved its targets until the early 1980s when things started to go wrong. Chairman Ray Stata decided to focus on performance measures such as product quality, on-time delivery, lead time, yields, and new-product time to market. But frustration with the slow rate of improvement led to the hiring of Schneiderman who knew that to be part of the reward system, quality goals needed to be realistic.

Schneiderman made an important discovery following a visit to one of Hewlett-Packard's Japanese plants which measured continuous improvement in terms of a 'half-life'. For each increment of time that equals this half-life, the defect level drops by 50 per cent. For example, if the initial defect level was 10 per cent and the defect half-life was six months, then after the first six months, the defect level would be down to 5 per cent, after the next six months it would be down to 2.5 per cent, and so on. Schneiderman decided to test his half-life concept at ADI. A scorecard of measures was established which included specific targets for seven key performance measures over a five-year period (see Figure 5.3).

Stata believed that the challenge of making continuous improvements with nine- to twelve-month half-lives over an extended period was awesome. The first reaction of the organisation was to recoil from what looked like unrealistic objectives. But he took the view that if a company really cares about its quality improvement objectives, there is no fundamental reason why these goals cannot be achieved. There were companies in Japan already operating at these levels on some of these measures. Over the next three years, on-time deliveries improved from

	1987	1992	Half-life (months)
On-time delivery	85%	> 99.8%	9
Outgoing defect level	500 ppm	< 10 ppm	9
Lead time	10 weeks	< 3 weeks	9
Manufacturing cycle time	15 weeks	4–5 weeks	9
Process defect level	5000 ppm	< 10 ppm	6
Yield	20%	> 50%	9
Time to market	36 months	6 months	24

Figure 5.3   ADI half-life measures

70 per cent to 96 per cent, outgoing defects improved from 500 ppm to 50 ppm, and average yields from 26 to 51 per cent. But not everything was right at ADI. The management structure and the accounting systems began to undermine the progress being made.

The use of the balanced scorecard and the half-life measurement system at ADI enabled the company to make significant headway. But increasingly it hit problems due to the conflict between the traditional accounting system which collected costs by departments and cost centres, and the requirements of its (horizontal) performance measures. Moreover, failing to change the management structure and allow managers to develop their own measures detracted from its success.

BENCHMARKING

While it is certainly important for continuous improvement measures to be elevated to the highest level, it is equally important for managers to keep a close eye on what is happening within their own sector and indeed industry in general. In other words, firms need to ensure that they are not reducing cost and eliminating unnecessary activities more slowly than the competition, and that they are faster to market than their nearest competitors. As one senior executive noted:

A revenue increase of 15% over last year and 5% ahead of budget is not such good news when the market grew 30% and our leading competitor increased sales by 40%.

This means that both internal and external data are needed to determine performance measures.

The derivation of external data is often achieved by the process of benchmarking. This entails analysing in detail the performance of companies deemed to be 'best in class' in performing certain processes and activities. Moreover, these companies need not necessarily be in the same industry as the analysing company. The focus is on the ability to perform selected activities well, such as billing, distribution, providing customer service and using suppliers as partners. Thus recently PepsiCo benchmarked, among others, British Airways, not because of the airline's supreme ability to sell soft drinks or fried chicken, but because its focus on providing excellent customer service was thought by PepsiCo to be worth emulating. Other recent examples of successful benchmarking include:

❑ the improvement in handling service calls within Rank Xerox as a result of benchmarking with the RAC and British Gas, who both had strong reputations in this area
❑ the improvement in the services provided on British Airways frequent flier programmes through its discussions with the Oriental Hotel in Bangkok – renowned for pampering its guests – on how to record details on customer preferences
❑ the reduction to eight minutes in the speed with which British Rail cleans its trains after benchmarking with similar activities on British Airways

Benchmarking seems to make a great deal of sense, but many companies have been reticent about giving outsiders information on some of their 'secrets'. However, those companies giving information are also usually those companies seeking information, so the learning process works both ways. Benchmarking is now a fast growing activity in itself but, to be effective, it requires a formal methodology. Organisations should have a clear idea of their own critical success factors (e.g. reduction in cycle time or excellent customer service) and knowledge of their own processes before they start to benchmark. As Lawrence Bossidy, CEO of Allied Signal, said in a recent interview:

> Benchmarking is not industrial tourism. It is looking at specific practices, getting the benefit of expertise, bringing it back, and having no inhibitions about adopting it and letting people know where it came from.

In 1981 Xerox launched a recovery programme largely based on employee involvement and benchmarking. Some of its main difficulties were concentrated in its warehousing operations which were a major source of problems leading to dissatisfied customers. Xerox managers decided to benchmark its warehousing systems with those of L.L. Bean, a mail-order distribution company operating in an entirely different industry whose distribution systems and expertise were well recognised.

Astounded by the level of speed and efficiency in Bean's operations, Xerox wasted no time in implementing a similar system within its own distribution operation. From that point on Xerox has been hooked on benchmarking. Between 1989 and 1992 the manufacturing division alone conducted no less than 200 benchmarking exercises and many of the larger units employ a full-time benchmarking manager. Such exercises have helped Xerox gradually recover its strength and profitability. Between 1984 and 1988, for example, customer satisfaction increased by 38 per cent, labour overhead decreased by 50 per cent and materials overhead decreased by 40 per cent.

REWARD SYSTEMS AND EMPLOYEE SUPPORT

Traditional performance measures tend to be based on financial information, and address the needs of shareholders and company executives. Moreover, these executives often have an increasing percentage of their compensation packages geared to this type of financial performance (e.g. share options and profit-related bonuses). Financial measures are also used lower down the management order as the basis for employee incentives and bonuses.

It might justifiably be asked why non-financial measures are not more widely used as the basis for incentives. Certainly the language of the workplace may be an inhibitor. And no amount of executive rhetoric about quality or customer satisfaction will easily change this, particularly if rewards remain attached to financial performance. However, some firms are making a move in this direction. For instance, IBM moved its sales incentive scheme for 1994 towards measures of customer profitability. It has geared 60 per cent of sales commissions to customer profits – the other 40 per cent is geared to some measure of customer satisfaction.

However, it is not only the type of reward system which is in question but whether reward systems work at all. While it is probably true that most managers intuitively believe incentive schemes to be a 'good thing', the empirical evidence from several studies suggests that they don't work! Alfie Kohn is one writer who believes that not only do incentive schemes not work, they:

> typically undermine the very processes they are intended to enhance... Research suggests that, by and large, rewards succeed at securing one thing only: temporary compliance. When it comes to producing lasting change in attitudes and behaviour, however, rewards like punishment, are strikingly ineffective... They do not create an enduring commitment to any value or action. Rather incentives merely – and temporarily – change what we do... As for productivity, at least two dozen studies over the last three decades have conclusively shown that people who expect to receive a reward for completing a task or for doing that task successfully simply do not perform as well as those who expect no reward at all.

In Kohn's view, rewards buy temporary compliance, so they appear to work. Many studies have shown that employees care more about training, the workplace environment and satisfied customers than about pay and rewards. Other studies have shown that profit participation (particularly through shareholding) is the way to build a strong, loyal and committed workforce. Nevertheless, no matter what the evidence against the effectiveness of incentive schemes, it is a brave manager who is prepared to scrap one.

Managers must also be careful when introducing new measurement systems. Middle managers are sometimes overwhelmed with the speed of change and often complain of 'measurement overload'. In FMC, a $4 billion US conglomerate, divisional managers were heard to say on the introduction of yet another improvement initiative: 'How is that supposed to fit in with the six other things we're supposed to be doing?' And not only that. According to CEO Larry Brady:

> Corporate staff groups were perceived by operating managers as pushing their pet programs on divisions. The diversity of initiatives, each with its own slogan, created confusion and mixed signals about where to concentrate and how the various programs interrelated. At the end of the day, with all these new initiatives, we were still asking division managers to deliver consistent short-term financial performance.

THE PROBLEMS WITH NON-FINANCIAL MEASURES AND SCORECARDS

The popularity of non-financial measures and scorecards is on the increase, and rightly so, for they take companies in the right measurement direction – towards the customer. But some critics have argued that the balanced scorecard is predominantly a top management tool of the 'command and control' school. This is not to say that the measures it emphasises are wrong, but it suggests that they are being used in the wrong way. The essence of this argument is that in a team-based structure, measures should be agreed and monitored by the teams – not by top management. In fact, if superiors start to interfere on the basis of evidence from their own measures (by, for example, demanding changes) the whole delicate edifice of the team-based system might well be undermined and could possibly collapse.

Fisher studied the effectiveness of non-financial measures at five American high-technology companies. They were all disenchanted with their existing measurement systems which were based around standard costing procedures. Variance reports arrived too late and the process of standard setting undermined any attempts at continuous improvement (managers soon realised that by helping raise the standards they were making life more difficult for themselves). Each company decided to measure customer satisfaction, reliability, responsiveness and quality, but in many cases selection of specific measures proved difficult. For example, to measure quality they used a combination of outgoing quality rates, customer rejections and warranties.

The implementation of these measures was judged only to be a qualified success. The chosen measures were clearly understood by managers and workers and action could usually be taken in some form or other at the plant level. But there were also other problems in implementation, many of which managers had not confronted before. For example, what measure of improvement should be targeted? Where should responsibility for achieving targets lie? Can suitable measures be found for knowledge and service work? And can the results of non-financial measures be translated into financial gains and losses?

The extent of these problems seriously impaired progress at the five firms. In particular, they found it difficult to tie together non-financial measures and profits, and consequently they were unsure whether the non-financial measures impacted the bottom line. As Fisher noted:

> The inability to quantify changes in terms of their effects on profits detracts from the impact of non-financial systems. Indeed, much of the uncertainty that exists about non-financial measures would dissipate if such a linkage were possible.

While it might be difficult to find any self-respecting manager who disagrees with the twin objectives of total quality and 100 per cent customer satisfaction, are these always compatible with maximising long-term profitability? As Eccles and Pyburn have suggested:

Is there a point where improvements in quality no longer lead to increased customer satisfaction? And is there a point where improvements in customer satisfaction no longer lead to increased profitability? Do trade-offs have to be made?

Financial and non-financial measures make uncomfortable bedfellows. For example, they often report conflicting short-term results. Take the case of additional investment in new machinery to improve manufacturing cycle time. Although this is likely to show a negative impact on short-term profits, the benefits – both in money and in time – are less easy to measure. Another example is the shipping of high-margin products at the end of an accounting period at the expense of standard lower-margin products. This results in a gain to the profit and loss account but has a negative effect on on-time delivery schedules and thus on customer satisfaction. Nor do non-financial measures, taken in isolation, always encourage the right behaviour. For example, if workers are rewarded for the percentage of on-time shipments, it makes sense to delay one large shipment in order to deliver ten smaller ones on time (given that they had already suffered the initial penalty).

MEASURES SHOULD BE SET BY TEAMS

While executives have the responsibility for setting strategy, in the horizontal organisation teams are the primary unit of execution. Indeed it is process teams which accept most of the responsibility and accountability for customer-oriented performance. Teams do the 'real' value-creating work. It is therefore crucial that the right team-based measures are chosen. The following four guiding principles are important in choosing a successful team-based performance measurement system:

❑ *Team-based measures should primarily help the team rather than provide a system of reporting up the line.* Team-based measures should not be created for top management to control the team, but to guide the team towards its process-based targets. Top managers have an important role to play in ensuring that team-based targets are synchronised with strategy, but the issue of 'management authority' needs to be carefully handled. According to Meyer:

> The team and senior managers should also set boundaries, which, if crossed, will signal that the team has run into trouble serious enough to trigger an 'out-of-bounds' management review. Such an approach keeps managers informed without disenfranchising the team... It must be clear that the purpose of the reviews is for senior managers to help the teams solve problems, not to find fault.

❑ *Teams should discuss their measurement needs and play a decisive role in developing their chosen measures.* The choice of team-based measures should not be made in isolation. The issue of ownership and accountability is central to the success of any measurement system, and this is no less true for team-based measures. It is the responsibility of senior managers to set strategic goals, ensure that teams understand their role in the strategic framework, and help teams devise their own measures. Departments at Milliken, for example, choose for themselves what to measure by deciding what is important to them and to the business. But it is important to ensure that ownership of and accountability for performance remain with the team.

❑ *Team-based measures should focus on the customer.* Because organisations tend to be structured by function, their measurement systems are usually concerned with functional performance. But team-based structures are concerned with delivering value to the customer, and therefore managers need to devise new measures to track this process. The old parochial thinking must be discarded and replaced by new measures of performance. Many firms have evolved a 'new' measurement language which has become part of their day-to-day conversation. One of the challenges that teams have to overcome is to make a clean break with the past, and this includes breaking with the old measurement vocabulary – but this is often easier said than done. Bernard Fournier of Rank Xerox recently explained this dilemma:

We have a whole language about measures which has been built up during the last 20 years and everyone is familiar with the jargon. Sometimes, this reinforces our internal orientation, not our customer responsiveness. Too many measures become permanent and that's the last thing we need. What we actually need are the right measures and frequently it is difficult to determine what these are.

❏ *Teams should choose only those measures that influence behaviour.* There is a real danger in all measurement systems that too many measures create a 'fog' through which it is difficult to see the real performance issues. Meyer reckons that any team-based measurement system should have a maximum of 15 measures. When functional members are brought together in a cross-functional team, they bring not only their functional expertise to the issues at hand, they also (often unwittingly) bring their functional measures and their functional vocabulary. The temptation to accommodate these different measures and emphases is invariably strong – nobody wants to seem to be too dismissive of ideas – but it must be resisted. Otherwise the sheer amount of work involved in gathering data for these measures will tie up valuable time, with the predictable result that new measures are added willy nilly, and old ones are retained. GE typified this problem in the 1970s:

> The bureaucracy routinely emasculated top executives by overwhelming them with useless information and enslaved middle managers with the need to gather it... Briefing books had grown to such dense impenetrability that top managers simply skipped reading them. Instead, they relied on staffers to feed them 'gotchas' with which to intimidate subordinates at meetings.

Teams need to adopt measures which are appropriate to the objectives within the overall strategic plan. And because teams focus on the customer, they are in a prime position to fix broken processes and improve performance. Take the case of one company which had one key performance measure for its parts warehousing operation – the percentage of customer orders that were filled the first time (from existing inventory), or the 'first fill' rate. But when the firm reorganised into multifunctional teams and began to see the customer perspective, a different understanding of performance was quickly reached. The new team was given the task of improving the total service to the customer from breakdown to repair. The customers didn't care about 'first fill' rates. They were concerned about getting a fast solution to their problem, and the fact that a certain part was in stock or not was not particularly relevant to this solution.

The new team began to analyse the way that service to the customer was provided, and looked at all the steps in the process, from the receipt of the order to the receipt by the customer (the dealer) of the part. Cycle times were measured for each step in the service cycle and then the team devised methods of reducing this time, while maintaining quality. New information systems and performance measures were then introduced to monitor and improve on these cycle times. The results were a reduction in paperwork, fewer delays in authorisation, improved quality, better delivery times, and a dramatic reduction in dealer complaints.

TOWARDS A NEW MEASUREMENT FRAMEWORK

Measurement systems have come a long way in recent years. From a narrow focus on financial numbers to sophisticated surveys of customer satisfaction, anything and everything is now being measured. Some critics of current practice frequently argue that firms have too many performance measures, many of which are hangovers from mergers and takeovers and stem from different measurement 'languages'. Notwithstanding all these important developments, financial measures have retained their primacy where it counts – in the boardroom and the investment community. In fact, in an investment world populated by computer networks programmed to take instant decisions based on the latest information, it is not surprising that financial measures are tightening their grip. This is placing even greater pressure on managers to improve quarterly results and on accountants to improve their skills at presenting the numbers. But these numbers are the tip of the iceberg.

They don't tell the full story and investors are beginning to realise it.

Such is their disenchantment with traditional financial numbers that many investors and executives are now adapting these numbers to represent measures of value-adding performance. Companies such as Coca-Cola, Anheuser Busch and Quaker Oats are beginning to use a proxy measure known as 'economic value-added' or EVA. Under EVA principles the only bottom line that really matters is the one drawn after charging the full cost of capital. Peter Drucker has commented:

> Until a business returns a profit greater than its cost of capital it operates at a loss... Until then it does not create wealth, it destroys it. By that measurement, incidentally, few U.S. businesses have been profitable since World War II.

In other words, by deducting the full cost of capital from the accounting profit, shareholders can measure the real underlying increase in their wealth. This puts pressure on managers to manage their assets more efficiently. But EVA is only a more interesting way of using existing accounting numbers – it does not try to see under the surface into the real value-adding processes of the business.

However, developments like EVA show that investors are starting to place a premium on information regarding the amount of value added by the organisation, and this should send a clear message to senior managers. But the message is not being heard. Managers are preoccupied with a whole raft of improvement programmes which have absorbed their time and drained their energy. And, while it is undeniable that total quality, reengineering, activity-based management and the balanced scorecard have all contributed to an improving picture of organisational performance, the whole picture still lacks shape and focus. Ideas are colliding, not connecting.

Horizontal information systems provide a framework for the balanced scorecard. They are the missing piece in the measurement puzzle, but they set new challenges to accountants and systems designers. Activity analysis has pointed people in the right direction – the challenge they now face is to realise its full potential.

6

SELL PROFITABLE PRODUCTS AND SERVICES

Many enterprises [have adopted] novel accounting perspectives. These include activity-based costing, target costing, life-cycle costing and others. There is no recorded instance of any of these techniques fully resolving the problems they set out to tackle... Ultimately, no cost management approach can be deemed good or bad in generalised terms. Organisational context and managerial ethos play a large part in determining the worthwhileness of accounting approaches.

M Bromwich and A Bhimani

PRODUCT COSTING SYSTEMS ARE NOT ENDS IN THEMSELVES. THEY PROVIDE information which influences strategic decisions – which products to sell in which markets and to which customers. But traditional product cost calculations are less than useful in markets where producers have little influence over price. In this world it is prices which should determine costs. Only in rare instances can firms adopt a cost-plus approach to pricing (for example, when competing in niche markets with minimal competition). In competitive markets firms need to adopt a different approach. The traditional cost control emphasis must be replaced with one of continuous cost reduction throughout the value chain.

In Chapter 3 we argued that the revenue stream from the final consumer fed the whole value chain, and that each member of the chain had an interest in the end-user price and the composition of its total costs. The higher the final consumer price and the lower the aggregate costs, the more profit is available to share among all members of the chain. Most firms, however, are primarily concerned with their own costs and prices, and have failed to appreciate their role in this broader context.

Selling *profitable* products and services is primarily concerned with managing costs. This chapter examines how cost management approaches are evolving to deal with the new realities, and looks at various product costing techniques. It also examines how costs should relate to strategy and how cost management can be improved across the value chain.

FROM COST-LED PRICING TO PRICE-LED COSTING

Traditional costing systems were developed to satisfy the information needs of growing industrial companies during the first half of the twentieth century. Their objectives were to plan, control and report on costs and to help managers make decisions on product volume and mix, and also to set prices. These systems served their purposes when firms could reliably plan and sell what they produced at their chosen price, but are work less well in today's customer-driven marketplace.

The traditional costing model

The basic principle underlying most of the costing systems still used today entails an assumption about the behaviour of costs: costs are classified as either *variable* (they vary with volume, for example with output or revenue) or *fixed* (they don't vary with volume). This simple classification is the root of most costing systems. Finance managers construct their budgets on the basis of 'recovering' fixed costs, and production managers aim to maximise volume to meet these recovery targets and generate profits once the 'break-even' level has been passed. There is another way of saying this. As more units are produced, more fixed costs are 'recovered' or 'absorbed' by production. Thus managers often speak in terms of 'fixed overhead recovery' – meaning that if more units than expected in the budget are produced, the firm 'over-recovers' its fixed costs and unit costs fall, whereas if fewer units are produced, there is an under-recovery of fixed costs and unit costs rise. Most volume and many pricing decisions are based on these beliefs. But reality is intruding on the assumptions of this model in ways which challenge its entire plausibility.

Manufacturing companies usually control production costs by 'standard costing' methods. This generally means that variable costs plus an attributable proportion of overheads represent the total standard cost of producing a particular product. This standard cost is set at the start of a period according to a number of assumptions, including those relating to output, capacity, material usage, labour requirements, machine time, material prices and overheads. At periodic intervals, this standard cost is compared with the actual cost. Any variances are usually caused by price changes in materials or labour (price variances), or by producing products faster or slower than expected (efficiency variances). Overheads are normally charged to products according to some volume-based 'allocation' method such as labour hours or machine time.

This focus on *allocating* costs to products has prevented many finance managers from realising that the changing *mix* of costs is destroying the credibility of their models. Overheads have risen as a proportion of total costs and direct labour costs have fallen, but questions have seldom been asked about the causes of these changes. Consequently few managers have realised that overhead costs are increasingly driven not by volume but by scope and diversity, caused by a wide variety of customer demands, such as product customisation, special packaging, and extended service commitments. The speed and scale of these changes have caught many companies unawares and they have stretched the credibility of traditional overhead allocation methods to breaking point. This point was well put by one senior executive:

We've been brought up to manage in a world where burden rates (the ratio of overhead costs to labour costs) are 100% to 200% or so. But now some of our plants are running with burden rates of over 1000%. We don't even know what that means.

A simple version of the unit cost-plus model is shown in Figure 6.1. This compares the manufacturing cost elements of a typical product in the production-led world of the 1960s with the customer-driven world of the 1990s.

	1960s	1990s
Material cost	10.0	10.0
Labour cost	8.0	2.0
Energy cost	2.0	4.0
Variable cost	*20.0*	*16.0*
Allocated overhead cost	12.0	20.0
Total cost	*32.0*	*36.0*

Figure 6.1   Traditional costing model

The obvious difference between the cost elements of the calculations in Figure 6.1 is in the lower labour cost and higher overhead content of the 1990s model. This has resulted in the overhead 'burden' rate increasing from 150 per cent to 1000 per cent, and illustrates the increasingly arbitrary way that the traditional model works. Although labour represents a smaller and smaller proportion of total costs, it is still the predominant basis of allocating overheads. One recent study of American manufacturing companies found that 74 per cent were still using direct labour as the primary method of overhead allocation, even though direct labour accounted for less than 10 per cent of total product costs for the majority of respondent firms. Another larger US study reported 62 per cent of companies using the direct labour allocation method.

Why have overheads risen to such an extent when most finance departments have developed more sophisticated systems for managing costs? Miller and Vollmann have suggested that many overheads are simply not seen by finance managers until too late. In other words, in their efforts to maximise volume and reduce unit costs, managers have generated high levels of extra costs, often needed to patch up poor quality and inefficient production, and provide a wider range of products. In a manufacturing operation geared to long production runs and large batch sizes, few of these extra costs add value for the customer. The traditional model has treated them as adverse variances, and the response of the firm has been to pass them on to the customer in higher prices. The overhead levels of European and American manufacturers highlight this problem. One recent American study showed that across the spectrum of US industry manufacturing overhead averaged 35 per cent of production costs, whereas the comparable figure for Japanese companies was 26 per cent. These problems are encapsulated in an observation made by Jones and Womack when they recount what they discovered on a visit to a German auto plant:

> At the end of the assembly line was an enormous rework and rectification area where armies of technicians laboured to bring the finished vehicles up to the company's fabled quality standard. One third of the total effort involved in assembly occurred in this area. The German plant was expending more effort to fix the problems it had just created than the Japanese plant required to make a nearly perfect car each time.

The primary reason for the lower overhead costs of Japanese companies is that they have geared their manufacturing operations to deal with product variety, in some cases producing in lot sizes of one. According to Stalk, volume-related costs decline by 15 to 25 per cent each time output doubles, but in a traditional factory, as variety increases, costs also increase, usually at the rate of 20 to 35 per cent each time variety doubles. With this in mind Toyota developed the flexible manufacturing system. In a flexible system variety-driven costs increase more slowly as variety grows, whereas scale costs remain unchanged. As its inventor, Taiichi Ohno, said, the system was 'born of the need to make many types of automobiles, in small quantities with the same manufacturing process'.

Douglas Shinsato, a partner at Tohmatsu Touche Ross in Japan, has watched the obsession of western companies with overhead recovery systems and reckons that most of them have wasted their opportunities in the Far East for that reason. One company he cites is IBM, contending that its rigid cost accounting system prevented it from pricing its products flexibly enough to match its Japanese archrival, Fujitsu.

This mentality, however, is not confined to product costs. The costs of service functions such as accounting and information technology are no longer accepted quite so unquestioningly as a charge (however calculated) for which the customer must pay. Increasingly, these functions are being seen as services which must compete for business both inside and outside the firm. Therefore the method of collecting and charging their costs has become a major issue, with somewhat unpredictable results.

In 1983, the year before it was separated from AT&T, Bellcore decided to charge out its major service activities to other (internal) client companies. This change in policy focused the minds of the client companies (the users) on the impact of these prices on their own business. This led directly to client company researchers doing their own word-processing (the word-processing services were too expensive) and to engineers making up their own slides and technical materials (the cost of the graphics departments was too high). Once deregulated, the client companies compared the prices charged by internal service providers with similar prices on the market. As external market prices were often much cheaper, internal service departments found themselves with fewer clients but with the same costs, which of course (following their overhead recovery mentality) resulted in an increase in their chargeout rates, leading to even fewer clients. In other words, they were pricing themselves out of work because they failed to understand the insidious effect which the volume-based allocation mentality was having on their business. Bellcore finally introduced a more sensible chargeout system which was accepted throughout the group, based on the actual resources consumed by the client companies.

The capacity problem

The overhead recovery mentality can also lead to management decisions which defy rationality. Consider the following situation. A consumer goods company recently launches a fifth type of kitchen knife. Production capacity is set at 90,000 units per month (the budget for the new product is 5000 units). But the new product doesn't sell and is quickly dropped from the range. What happens next? The automatic pilot of the cost allocation system moves into gear, and the capacity costs originally charged to the dropped product are reallocated to the four remaining products. The result is predictable (if difficult to credit) – the fourth product is now marginal. This downward or 'death spiral' can easily occur through blind adherence to an overhead recovery mentality.

Now imagine that a salesperson calls in with a firm order for 10,000 knives which require a slightly different design. The manager of the plant discusses the order with his finance manager. Both agree that they can design and produce the new knife, that they are already incurring the costs of labour and machinery whether or not the order is taken, and that the price, although keen, at least covers the direct costs of production. The decision appears to be obvious – take the order. But is it really so obvious?

If the order is accepted, what are other salespeople to think? Should they also take similar orders at keen prices provided these orders make a contribution to overheads? The answer is that if they do accept such orders the costs that appear to be fixed in the short run will begin to increase (or the expenses currently incurred will be difficult to reduce). Once firms become embroiled in the business of taking incremental orders they need to expand their support resources, both inside and outside the factory. There are cost implications for design, scheduling, production, marketing, sales, distribution and service. Moreover, incremental business tends to place disproportionate demands on these resources and thus produces substantial diseconomies of scale.

The contribution margin approach (manifested in such phrases as, 'we can discount these airline seats, or theatre tickets, or hotel rooms to $x, provided we make some contribution to overheads') is equally prevalent in service businesses where the existence of excess capacity is even more apparent. Contribution analysis encourages and reinforces the mentality that there is always a good reason to add or retain a product, or service and seldom a good reason to abandon one. Equally, there is always a valid reason to accept a price which generates a contribution to overheads (however vaguely they are defined). But Shank, among others, regards contribution analysis – or as it is sometimes referred to, marginal costing – as a subtle, insidious snare. He was recently asked the classic contribution margin question: 'Suppose an airline has an empty seat on a flight leaving in one hour. Isn't the contribution approach appropriate for pricing that seat?' Shank replied:

> I understand as well as you the sense in which that extra seat is free. What I have said is that for my 25 years of experience, the mindset that will sell that seat for $50 because it is free destroys companies. We have created the mindset that profit at that level is real profit.

Activity-based costing

Peter Drucker put his finger on the traditional product costing problem way back in 1963:

> Now the only way the accountant can allocate costs is in a way that is proportionate to volume rather than proportionate to transactions. Thus one million in volume produced in one order – or in one product – carries the same cost as one million in volume production by one million individual orders, or by 50 production runs. The accountant is concerned with cost per unit of output, rather than the costs of a product. Most large companies typically end up with thousands of items in their product line – and all too frequently fewer than 20 really sell. However, these 20 items have to contribute revenues to carry the cost of 9,999 non sellers.

These inadequacies have persuaded managers to search for better ways of determining product costs. They have undoubtedly been stimulated by the work of Cooper and Kaplan, who have long championed the virtues of activity-based costing (ABC).

Ali suggests that ABC developed as a response to the pitfalls of both unit costing and contribution margin analysis – specifically, distorted product costs from the unit-cost model and a short-run orientation in the contribution margin model. Originally developed by industrial giants such as John Deere and Hewlett-Packard (where the technique is sometimes referred to as cost driver accounting), ABC attempts primarily to gain a clearer picture of product costs through a better identification of the costs of activities consumed by products, and secondarily, but perhaps more importantly, to provide clues as to whether such activities are necessary in the first place (do they add value for those who use them?). Johnson and Kaplan place the problem in context:

> Although simplistic product costing methods are adequate for financial reporting requirements...the methods systematically bias and distort costs of individual products. When such distorted information represents the only available data on 'product costs', the danger exists for misguided decisions on product pricing, product sourcing, product mix, and responses to vital products. Many firms seem to be falling victim to the danger.

The costs of some activities are relatively easy to identify with products, for example the use of raw materials, energy and, occasionally, direct labour. But tracing such activity costs as set-up time, materials requisitioning and inspecting the quality of incoming materials is much harder. Cooper and Kaplan suggest that by observing what really happens in factories, it becomes clear that many more so-called 'fixed' costs vary with production than traditional systems suggest. Identifying which costs are fixed, and which are variable, has puzzled accountants for years. Cooper and Kaplan recommend using the 'rule of one'.

> If only one person (or one machine) exists in a department, it can be considered a fixed expense. But when more than one unit of a resource exists in a department, it must be a variable resource. Something is creating a demand for the output from that department, and more than one unit of resource is required to satisfy that demand.

Cooper and Kaplan see activity costs as existing within a hierarchical structure. They suggest, for example, that in manufacturing there are different levels of activity within the hierarchy, and that a well-designed ABC system should recognise these different levels. Figure 6.2 shows the ABC model in a manufacturing setting. ABC traces 'fixed overhead' costs to units, batches, product lines and whole facilities, based on the activities which each level demands. There are, in other words, different levels of variability within the 'fixed overhead' structure. Thus individual units draw on batch level costs (set-ups, purchase orders, etc.); batches draw on product-sustaining costs (engineering change notices, etc.); and product-level activities draw on facility-sustaining costs (costs of buildings, etc.). This cascading method of cost attribution provides a more accurate (and more realistic) final product cost.

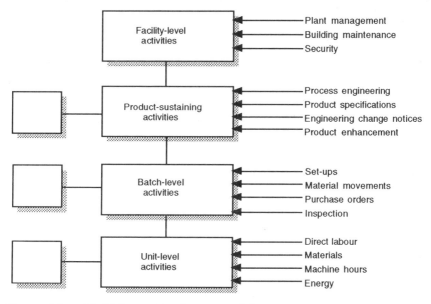

Figure 6.2   ABC hierarchical cost model

The application of ABC methods can have a significant impact on the costs of individual products. In 1989 Hewlett Packard implemented an ABC system at its Boise Surface Mount Centre (BSMC), in Idaho. Before adopting ABC, all overhead was applied to product costs according to the percentage of direct labour and material used. This led to predictable, but dangerous, behaviour by the design engineers. As the HP controller explained:

> The purpose of cost driver accounting [activity-based costing] was not to prevent the engineers from introducing new technology. Rather it was to get engineers to think about cost, and not go for elegance every time. Cost driver accounting put product costs on the backs of engineers. It encouraged them to design for manufacturability... Engineering was attacking the cost reduction problem by getting rid of labour. While that was a good goal, we were rapidly reaching the point of diminishing returns. For example, to get labour out of a product, they re-engineered it with many new components. What they were actually doing was driving more and more non-standard part numbers into manufacturing. So, every new product we introduced had a whole set of new part numbers.

The effects of ABC methods on the cost of the 57 products produced at the BSMC are shown in Figure 6.3.

Percentage change caused by ABC	Number of products
Over 100%	1
+50% to +100%	5
+20% to +50%	6
+5% to +20%	23
−5% to +5%	13
−20% to −5%	9
TOTAL	57

Figure 6.3   Change in product costs using ABC methods

Hewlett-Packard has used various forms of ABC since the mid-1980s. As Paré explains, in HP's fast-changing high-tech world, the life cycle of a product can be briefer than young love. The ABC data, which tally the costs of all the activities required in manufacturing and distribution, quickly found their way into the desktop computers of HP's designers, enabling them to run sophisticated cost estimates of their ideas even as they are hatched. The company's hit products – new models of the HP 3000 and HP 9000 mid-range computers – were created by designers who had real-time cost information at their fingertips. When ABC showed that testing new designs and parts was extremely expensive, engineers changed their plans on the spot to favour components that required less testing, thus lowering costs. As Ronald Foster, HP's controller of manufacturing for computer systems, explains:

> They used to hand the design over to accountants who needed a couple of days to estimate the production cost. Then in some cases the designers would be told what they wanted was too expensive.

But, as Paré points out, HP is not stopping there. It continues to develop ABC techniques to assess the risk of innovation in a market with a short product life. The company usually spreads the excess costs of design innovation over all its products. The objective is not to discourage innovation but to improve risk assessment.

The introduction of ABC at the Malaysian plant of American semiconductor company Advanced Micro Devices also produced some surprises. Using the traditional costing model, AMD managers reckoned it cost no more than $2 to assemble and test its most expensive products and that 60 per cent of the company's goods cost only 25 cents each. But when ABC methods were applied they discovered that the more complicated, low-volume chips, which are more difficult to assemble and require more testing, cost far more to produce. ABC showed that 54 per cent of the company's products cost at least 75 cents to make, and some chips cost as much as $3.50. They soon changed their product mix and prices to reflect this new-found reality.

Drucker suggests that had Ford, Chrysler and GM used ABC, they would have realised the utter futility of their competitive blitzes of the past few years, which offered new car buyers spectacular discounts and hefty cash rewards. He points out that these promotions actually cost the big three automakers enormous amounts of money and, worse, enormous numbers of potential customers. In fact, every one resulted in an unwelcome drop in market standing. But neither the costs of the special deals nor their negative yields appeared in the companies' conventional cost accounting figures, so managers never saw the damage. The big Japanese automakers – Toyota, Nissan and Honda – all use some form of ABC (although primitive), and this was sufficient to tell them not to compete with the US automakers through discounts, thus maintaining their market share and profitability.

While ABC has been a significant step forward in the search for more accurate product costs, it has not proved to be the panacea its advocates first suggested. A recent report commissioned by the Chartered Institute of Management Accountants in the UK, for example, considered the usefulness of ABC, but while acknowledging its value in certain cases, found the overall arguments for change unconvincing. The authors of the report went on to say:

> Current evidence and experience suggest that those who urged the use of ABC as a revolutionary approach to accounting likely to cause a whole-sale change in extant accounting systems have not yet provided a sufficiently strong case or the necessary empirical evidence to convince practitioners.

The application of ABC systems frequently runs into problems of data collection and lack of integration with the financial system. For these reasons Ness and Cacuzza estimate that as many as 90 per cent of ABC projects fail to last the course. Nanni, Dixon, and Vollmann have argued:

> Our exposure to some 20 organisations that have recently begun activity-based analysis programmes, [shows that they all] ultimately decided not to actually install a complete ABC system, since the vast majority of the benefits, they believe, are to be found in the analysis itself.

Price-led costing

Existing cost management approaches (whether activity based or not) concentrate excessively on the attribution of internally generated costs to products. This very focus leaves them vulnerable to other external influences. In other words, there is little virtue in having an excellent costing system which accurately plots product costs to three decimal places, if the actual product costs are much higher than those of competitors. Some organisations, having recognised this, are now moving from 'cost-led pricing' to 'price-led costing'.

To remain competitive firms must undoubtedly continue to reduce costs, but knowing where to focus attention for maximum benefit is not always clearly understood. For example, some firms have developed huge centralised purchasing departments which concentrate primarily on reducing the costs of direct materials, whereas the greatest potential for cost savings occurs before products or services are committed to the marketplace. One technique which has gained favour in recent years is *target costing*. Its extensive use by Japanese manufacturers has contributed much to its growth in popularity.

The contrast between traditional and target costing approaches is set out in Figure 6.4. The traditional model starts with the product specification provided by the design and engineering departments. The accountants then apply costs to each component and add the required profit margin to arrive at the projected price. As Steven Hronec of Arthur Andersen put it: 'US companies mainly just add up the pieces'. If the market price is judged too high they go back around the same loop until either a different design (with lower costs) is produced, or the product idea is accepted with a lower profit margin or dropped altogether.

The target costing model takes a different view. Japanese manufacturers typically start with a target cost based on the price the market is prepared to accept. Then they tell designers and engineers to meet it. Target costs are set for every product component, and suppliers are invited to tender on the basis of such costs. If suppliers have a problem in meeting a particular target cost, they either redefine the product specification within new cost guidelines, or they meet with their own suppliers to work out a mutually acceptable way of reducing costs. However, what doesn't change is the target cost. All members of the value chain are thus involved in solving cost issues, the incentive being the guarantee of work by the principal manufacturer.

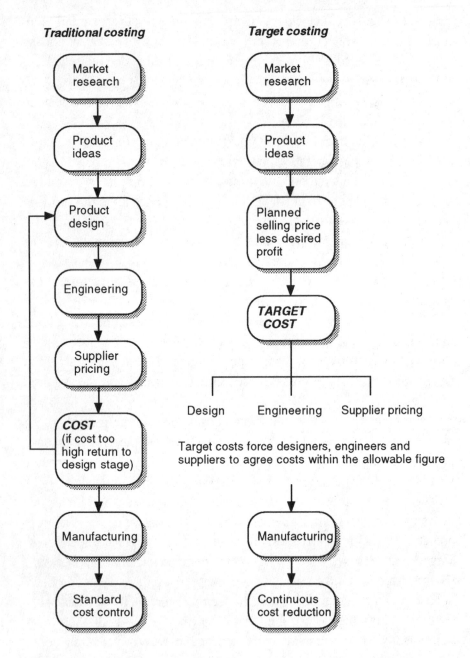

Figure 6.4   Comparison of traditional costing with target costing approach

The critical factor in target costing is its focus on reducing product costs at the design and development stage, i.e. before the product is committed to production. Once the target cost has been achieved, low unit costs are not dependent on high volume production runs. And without the intense pressure created by numerous production changes, companies can develop more stable production processes, operate flexibly, produce only what is demanded, and concentrate on high quality production. In other words, by managing costs at the design and development stage, they minimise the struggle throughout the production process to keep costs within budget. The focus is on the speed of attaining the target cost, and not on a regular comparison of actual costs with (obsolete) budgets. The results of this approach are, usually, lower inventories and more satisfied customers.

The target costing approach puts less emphasis on such cost classifications as 'fixed' and 'variable'. Rather, it seeks to minimise total costs through the value chain. A number of western car manufacturers such as Mercedes-Benz and Chrysler have now adopted the target costing approach. For example, in a recent interview, Mercedes-Benz CEO Helmut Werner said that 'Mercedes now has to produce cars to match market-driven prices, not make the autos its engineers design at whatever the cost'.

Japanese car manufacturers have built an enviable reputation for bringing new products to market on time and at the right cost. Their methods of target costing and supplier management are at the root of this success. But how does it really work? The answer, in Toyota's case, is by painstaking professionalism. Toyota and its key suppliers help each other cut lead times and reduce costs. However, there is a popular misconception that all front-line suppliers are classed as business partners. The reality is that of the 100–200 first-tier suppliers, only a dozen or so are elevated to the rank of partner (and share technology, strategy and information). The rest are given specific roles.

Toyota's suppliers know what is expected of them in, for example, new product development. Relevant development ideas are presented 36 months prior to production, but once a concept has been approved (27 months prior to production) there is little latitude for further changes.

From that point on – through the prototyping stage – milestones have to be met and target costs and performance levels reached. The whole network of supply is tightly coordinated: any slippage in targets at one level could have damaging effects elsewhere. There is little sympathy for missed targets.

Business partners can discuss and negotiate targets in the pre-production phase. Toyota submits targets four months after the initial supplier presentation and small improvements are usually requested, such as a 4 per cent reduction in cost or a 5 per cent improvement in performance. But while these performance improvements are stressed quite forcibly, suppliers understand that there is some element of flexibility. Toyota also sends suppliers a broad specification showing how parts must interact with those of other suppliers. Unlike many western car manufacturers which increasingly rely on computer-aided design, Toyota still places a high value on prototyping to finalise the specification and gain the commitment of suppliers to meet target costs.

Value analysis, as illustrated in Figure 6.5, is an activity which helps to design products to meet the needs of customers at the lowest cost and with the highest standards of quality and reliability. It is used extensively in target costing, especially in what is known as 'functional analysis'. This process determines the function of each part of the product and attempts to match the functional cost with the perceived customer value, thus helping to evaluate the target cost. Sometimes this can involve five or ten reviews which can take the form of two- or three-day sessions where internal and external advisers meet to thrash out cost reduction strategies.

Such an approach was a culture shock for managers at a new Suzuki plant in Hungary. Laszlo Pataki commented:

> They taught me to concentrate on every detail and ask how to do it cheaper. That was not part of the Hungarian culture. We were never taught value engineering.

Target costing is not without its problems. One recent study of Japanese companies suggested that one of the major difficulties is deciding on the

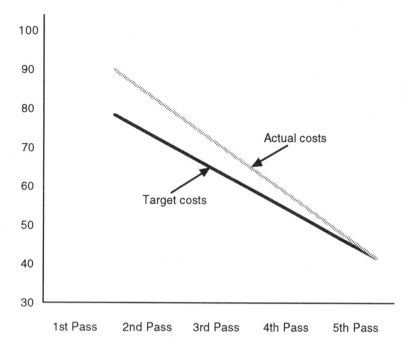

Figure 6.5   Value analysis method of cost reduction

tightness of the targets in terms of the effort required to obtain them. Another problem concerns the level in the cost hierarchy at which targets should be set. The respondents in this study indicated that 41 per cent set a target cost for each level, 39 per cent at the product level and 16 per cent at the product group level.

Target costing is used extensively by Japanese firms, but this does not negate the need to monitor actual costs. In fact, most Japanese firms operate some form of standard costing, including the allocation of over-heads to products on the basis of direct labour. However, the purpose of these systems is different from that of most western counterparts. Standard cost systems are used as a basis for cost reduction rather than as a means of determining prices or supporting other managerial deci-sions. And, although the direct labour allocation method is recognised to be arbitrary, Japanese managers look on this as a means of minimising labour costs rather than deriving product costs.

STRATEGIC COST MANAGEMENT

One of the more recent (and more relevant) criticisms of management accounting is that it looks only at what is happening inside the firm. In other words, it concentrates on measuring immediate inputs (purchases, costs, assets) and immediate outputs (sales, revenues and cash flow), whereas a broader understanding of the whole value chain (in which a particular firm is only a part) gives managers a better understanding of the competitive position (and opportunity) of the firm. This criticism has led to the development of strategic cost management. Bromwich terms this strategic management accounting, which he defines as:

> The provision and analysis of financial information on the firm's product markets and competitors' costs and cost structures and the monitoring of the enterprise's strategies and those of its competitors in these markets over a number of periods.

The aim of strategic cost management is to align costs with strategy and its methodology is concerned with matching the cost of work in the value chain with the value provided to the final customer. Companies need to understand their strategic cost drivers and work to reduce them relative to those of their competitors.

The concept of the value chain was discussed in Chapter 3. Competing firms have different value chains. For example, in the oil industry different firms specialise in exploration, production, refining, distribution and retailing. Some vertically integrated firms cover all these stages. But the final consumer price governs all costs and margins within the chain. Moreover, these costs and profit margins impact on each other, reflecting competitive pressures and relative bargaining strengths. The shift in the balance of power from suppliers to large retailers in the UK, for example, has been very evident in recent years.

As already explained, in traditional management theory (and practice) cost is a function of volume. However, from a strategic perspective there are many factors, which are often interrelated, that cause costs. These costs can be classified as structural (driven by technology, scale, experience and complexity), or executional (quality, design, customer service and innovation).

The turnaround at Ford between 1981 and 1994 shows how an acute awareness of both structural and executional cost drivers can contribute to success. In 1981, Ford was a poor second to General Motors. It produced half the cars, and was outgunned on every front – scale, investment in technology, marketing and vertical integration. Through the 1980s GM invested $45 billion in new manufacturing plants which included the latest computer integrated manufacturing equipment. However, by analysing its cost drivers Ford found a weak spot at GM – product line complexity. It realised that GM's product options to the customer (models, body types and options packages) involved literally billions of combinations, and that the cost implications for GM must be horrendous.

Ford used this new knowledge to develop a different strategy. By reducing the number of models and offering combined factory-installed options (as did Honda and Toyota), Ford gained a huge cost advantage. Moreover, the new GM plants were a nightmare – in fact (owing to low labour morale and high complexity) unit costs were lower in the older less technology-driven plants. Ford also saw another weakness in one of GM's executional cost drivers – manufacturing quality. Ford attacked this area and through its 'Quality is Job One' programme made great gains in market share over the next few years.

Wal-Mart's meteoric rise in recent years is legendary, but it was achieved largely through a clear understanding of the cost drivers within its value chain. Wal-Mart saw an opportunity to reduce costs in its warehousing capabilities by developing a technique known as 'cross-docking', under which goods are delivered continuously to the warehouses where they are selected, repacked, and then dispatched to stores, often without spending any time in stock. In other words,

Wal-Mart was able to achieve economies of scale without the usual attendant inventory and   handling costs. By using this system Wal-Mart was able to reduce costs by 2 to 3 per cent and defeat its rivals in the battle for 'everyday low prices'.

Managing costs across the value chain can pay rich dividends. Japanese companies realised many years ago that by helping suppliers improve their business they would, in turn, improve their own (and reduce their costs). Consider what happened at Toyota, where managers were dissatisfied with the response times of one particular component supplier, which was taking 15 days to produce and deliver a part. The first step was to cut the lot sizes, reducing response times to 6 days. The next step was for Toyota to streamline the layout of the supplier's factory, reducing the number of inventory holding points and cutting the response time again, to 3 days. Finally, Toyota eliminated all work in progress at the supplier's plant until its final target response time of 1 day was achieved.

Womack and Jones quote the example of Nissan (UK), where the delivery of poor quality parts severely disrupted the launch of the new Primera, its first car designed for the European market.

The normal action in the UK would have been to replace the 'problem' suppliers. Instead, Nissan's British purchasing department teamed up with the Nissan R & D centre to place supplier-development teams of Nissan engineers inside each supplier for extended periods to improve their key processes. Nissan's theory was that giving suppliers advice on meeting high standards would produce superior results. Two years later, when Nissan began production of the Micra, a new small car, this approach had transformed these suppliers from Nissan's worst into its best.

However, supply chain integration does not always work so well. In fact, if the effects of changes within one business on another are ignored, costs can be driven up. A few years ago one of the major American automobile companies decided to implement a just-in-time approach to inventory management in its assembly plants. Its manufacturing costs were 30 per cent of sales value. It estimated that this JIT approach would reduce its assembly costs by about 20 per cent, thus bringing its costs in line with those of similar Japanese firms. The initial results of the programme were excellent, with significant reductions in both inventories and cost. However, the reaction from suppliers caught the firm unawares. Because its suppliers were not organised for this rapid and regular delivery system, their costs went through the roof. But when the suppliers tried to recover these extra costs through higher prices, the auto firm informed them that this was not acceptable. Value chain analysis revealed the true picture.

When the costs and margins of the assembly firm and the parts supplier were seen as part of one chain, it became clear that the parts supplier was, in fact, adding more manufacturing value to the car than the assembly plant. When the assembly plant adopted its JIT policy, production scheduling at the supplying company went haywire, with a resultant dramatic increase in cost. This more than offset the cost savings from the JIT initiatives, causing the overall costs of the two firms to increase and combined profits to fall. Unlike its Japanese competitors, the American auto plants experienced large variations in production demand with the attendant impact on production scheduling. Only one week ahead of production, the master schedule was 25 per cent wrong, 95 per cent of the time! In comparison, Japanese plants varied 1 per cent or less from schedules laid down four weeks in advance. This lack of communication with suppliers cost the American auto plants dearly, and led to a rethinking of policy.

The lesson is clear. Major changes of policy should not be made without taking account of their effects throughout the value chain. Partnerships exist (implicitly or explicitly) between firms within the value chain, but these should not be seen as barriers to internal changes – rather they represent opportunities to be explored for mutual benefit. Many Japanese firms have gained significant market share through an understanding of these intricacies and interdependencies.

Benefits can also be gained at the customer end of the chain. Most industrial companies define the customer as the party to whom they sell their products. Their analysis and commitment stop at this point. But Gouillart and Sturdivant have pointed out that this is a serious mistake:

This failure to listen carefully to all customers, to empathise with their needs and desires, results in reduced service levels, streamlined product lines, and uniform product designs. It inadvertently favours cost reduction at the expense of individuality, even when market needs point towards greater customisation. What's more, managers who are not market focused often come to the conclusion that there is really no fundamental difference between their offering and that of their competitors. Commoditisation, the natural outgrowth of all competitors fighting with the same weapons, becomes a self fulfilling prophecy. And commoditisation is why so many industrial companies that embraced time-based competition or reengineering may have realised short term gains but have ended up destroying their industries' profit margins... Top-level managers need to spend a day in the life of key customers in their distribution chains. There is no substitute for managers' instincts, imagination and personal knowledge of the market. It should be the essence of corporate strategy.

Strategic cost management also entails an understanding of the *internal value chain*, and in particular of how costs are incurred over the life cycle of a product. Japanese VCR manufacturers, for example, were able to reduce the unit costs of their products from $1300 in 1977 to $298 in 1984 by understanding how better design (resulting in fewer parts) reduced production costs. The technical director of Xerox Corporation made this point:

One of the things we are starting to understand is that the ability to control costs is largely determined before the item gets into production...yet all our cost management is focused after production, when we have 10–20% control over costs...so we try to influence the product costs by influencing the design part of the product.

A typical product life cycle shows that up to 85 per cent of all production and pre-production costs are committed by the end of the design stage. This suggests that attempts to control costs during the production stage (e.g. by shaving material prices and reducing direct labour costs) may be futile. Figure 6.6 shows that the stages at which costs are actually spent does not correspond with the stages at which

% Life cycle costs

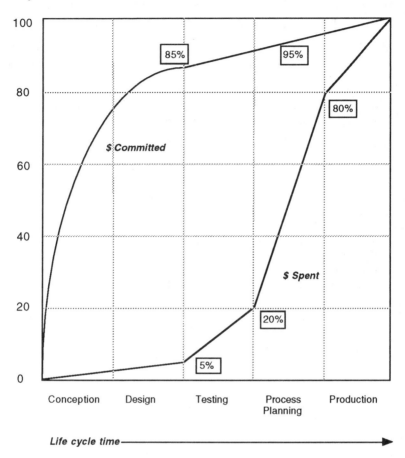

Figure 6.6   Product life cycle graph

they are committed. Thus most of the cash is spent on set-up, planning, and the production process. Moreover, as managers start to understand that the speed of design and production is now crucial to cost minimisation, they must ensure that their cost systems are aligned with this thinking. Meyer recently commented:

The manufacturing cycle for a car is less than a day, whereas development cycle time for a new automobile in the United States is approximately 48 months. By moving fast cycle time upstream, one begins to achieve significant leverage. The root cause of major manufacturing cycle time improvement begins with product and process design. Design for manufacturability and design for assembly provide enormous leverage to reduce manufacturing cycle time.

Errors or delays in one part of the value chain can multiply if not caught early enough. This 'snowballing effect' can be costly – a factor of ten has even been suggested in product development. One study, focused on a major electrical product in each phase of development, noted the accumulated cost of errors as represented by such a factor (see Figure 6.7).

Error corrected	Cost
At the design stage	$1,000
At the testing stage	$10,000
At the process planning stage	$100,000
At the test production stage	$1,000,000
At the final production stage	$10,000,000

Figure 6.7   Factor of ten in product development

These costs are, however, negligible compared with the costs of fixing errors discovered in the marketplace. The failure to detect an error with the rotary compressor component of a refrigerator cost GE $400 million. Only later did the company find that a number of its technical people were unhappy with the long-term reliability of the parts at the outset.

Much management effort at cost reduction is misguided. For example, many firms believe that competitive tendering is one of the most powerful ways to reduce costs. But the 'cost savings' created through competitive tendering are often more apparent than real. This type of 'adversarial' approach tends to ignore the possible benefits which come from a close customer–supplier relationship where, when the chips are down, the supplier does everything possible to help the customer. Competitive tendering, which emphasises price, tends to work against this sort of relationship.

Some companies impute different 'overhead' costs to bought-in items according to their source. At one of the Hewlett-Packard plants in the UK, for example, managers have calculated that the cost of the purchasing 'overhead' depends entirely on its source. Internally produced parts are the least expensive, those bought from a multinational partner more expensive, and those bought from a local firm dearest of all. According to Jim Rigby, controller at HP's plant in Scotland:

> We were able to tell engineers that it costs 18 cents to procure components from a multinational partner with corporate price agreements, EDI, no inspection, etc., versus a local supplier with low volumes where the procurement costs can be as much as 50 per cent of the purchase value of the material unit costs.

Once again, the causes of costs are not immediately, or intuitively, obvious. The relationships between investments, prices, costs and profits are extremely complex. It is only by understanding, and managing, costs in a strategic context that managers will be able to come to terms with these issues.

7

FIND AND RETAIN
PROFITABLE CUSTOMERS

*It is common for a business to lose 15% to 20% of its customers each
year. Simply cutting defections in half will more than double the average
company's growth rate.*

Frederick Reichheld and W Earl Sasser Jr

ORGANISATIONS MAY PROVIDE EXCELLENT SERVICE AND MANAGE THEIR
businesses efficiently, but unless the revenue they receive from
customers is greater than the costs of providing products and services,
such attributes will count for little.

That a customer is profitable cannot be taken for granted. Each
customer draws on the resources of the organisation in a different way.
Some are inexpensive to serve and some are very demanding. Some are
prepared to pay extra for good service, whereas others demand excellent
service, fast delivery and low prices as of right. Relationships also
change over time. For example, as noted in the previous chapter, the
balance of power has shifted dramatically from suppliers to large retailers in recent years. Wal-Mart, Toys 'R Us, Sainsbury and Marks and
Spencer demand the earth from suppliers (and usually get it), but they

are not prepared to pay premium prices. Suppliers must keep their customer strategies under constant review. Johnson emphasised the point in this way:

> To achieve competitive and profitable operations in a customer-driven global economy, companies must give customers what they want, not persuade them to purchase what the company now produces at the lowest cost. If customers favour frequent delivery of small lots, or if they favour smaller-sized products, then companies must respond accordingly – even when it initially costs more.

FINDING PROFITABLE CUSTOMERS

The question of customer profitability is surrounded by myths and false premises. Some managers, for example, believe that provided the gross profit from sales (which *can* usually be measured) contributes to 'fixed' overheads, no further analysis of the customer relationship is necessary. But, as we noted in Chapter 6, far more so-called 'fixed costs' vary with customer demands than might first be imagined. Presale costs vary according to size, importance, distance, resources employed to win the order, visits, demonstrations, quotations and so forth. Production costs vary by order size, design, customisation, special packaging and inventory levels. Distribution costs vary according to distance, speed and mode of transport. Post-sale costs differ according to installation, training, support, warranty provisions and future maintenance. Activity analysis has shown that as much of 60 per cent of sales value can be related to customer-driven costs.

That there is such a variation in customer-driven costs is not surprising. The problem is that prices rarely take account of such variations. Differences in price (excluding quantity discounts) for the same product and for similar transactions can be as much as 30 per cent, but such differences bear little relationship to the costs of serving the customer. Myer has suggested that in fast-moving consumer goods industries the costs of selling, buying, trade marketing, delivering and paying for the product represent between 20 and 40 per cent of the consumer price, and that 25 to 50 per cent of these costs are unnecessary.

Nor can managers always tell intuitively which of their customers are profitable. Indeed, research suggests that up to 70 per cent of customers are not profitable at all. And what's more surprising is that it is often the larger customers who represent the biggest losses. This state of affairs may be bad enough when orders are plentiful, but in times of intense competition and wafer-thin margins, lack of knowledge of customer profitability is a recipe for disaster. Evidence on the extent of the variation within customer and channel profitability is mounting. Five recent studies all reveal a similar profitability pattern.

The first study, of a pharmaceutical distribution company, showed that only 30 per cent of customers were profitable; this 30 per cent generated 261 per cent of the profits (and the top 10 per cent, 151 per cent); and the remaining 70 per cent of customers managed to 'lose' 161 per cent of these profits. These findings followed the introduction of an ABC system. This system recorded costs by orders processed, order size, delivery to store, cartons shipped, and shelf stacking at the customer site. The study allowed managers to develop a menu pricing system and instigate (successful) efforts to drive down the costs of unnecessary activities.

Similar results were seen in the second study at Kanthal, a Swedish company which specialises in the production and sale of electrical resistance heating elements. It had 10,000 customers and 15,000 products. After detailed analysis of its Swedish customers (once again conducted on an activity basis), the profitability profile showed that only 40 per cent of customers were profitable. These customers generated 250 per cent of profits. More alarming were the extremes. The most profitable 5 per cent of customers brought in 150 per cent of the profits; the least profitable 10 per cent 'lost' 120 per cent of profits. Moreover, two of the most unprofitable customers proved to be among the top three in sales volume. The customer profitability profile of both the pharmaceutical and Kanthal studies was remarkably similar (see Figure 7.1).

Managing these 'extreme' customers – protecting the 'winners' and rethinking relationships with the 'losers' – became a managerial imperative. Indeed the customer analysis, in Kanthal's case, led to a

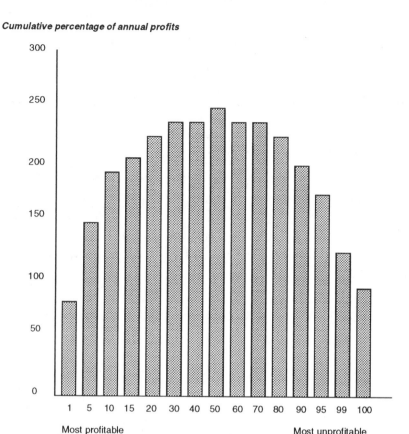

Figure 7.1   Approximate profitability distribution of pharmaceutical company and Kanthal studies

series of more strategic moves following the understanding that most of Kanthal's customer-related costs were driven by customer orders.

Thus Kanthal installed a direct on-line order entry system at the customer's location; converted one large, unprofitable customer (who had been placing lots of small orders) into a distributor; and, perhaps most dramatically, decreased prices for one customer by 5 per cent after the customer agreed to reduce the number of order lines by 50 per cent (the profit margin for this customer rose from 19 per cent to 45 per cent even with the price cut).

Kanthal's largest ever deal was based on information from its new customer profitability system. Price levels and 'standard behaviour' were agreed. Deviations, such as short-term changes to technical specifications and special delivery conditions, were to be charged extra. One of Kanthal's biggest customers, a major player in the US market, was so impressed with the system that Kanthal managers were invited to participate in seminars for other suppliers on the topic of building such systems and relationships.

The third study was carried out by a medium-sized UK distributor to the retail sector. The company provided a nationwide delivery service to 18,000 customers through more than 60 branches. The study revealed that only 70 per cent of customers were profitable; the cost of serving each of the least profitable 28 per cent was significantly greater than the gross margin they produced; and the largest customer (a major company representing 20 per cent of turnover) was generating large losses.

The fourth piece of work related to a company in the UK confectionery market in the late 1980s. Figure 7.2 shows the comparative profitability of the three main types of distribution channel at both the gross margin level and the net profit level. The analysis shows that when the resources used within each type of channel are applied under activity-based methods, the CTN, or confectionery/tobacconist/newsagent outlet, which generated by far the highest return on sales at the gross margin level made a significant loss at the net margin level (i.e. after identifying appropriate distributing, selling, marketing and financing costs). Nor was it profitable for the company to sell through the multiple (i.e. supermarket/hypermarket) channel after customer-related costs were charged. In fact, all the organisation's profit came from the 'wholesale' channel. Once again, strategic questions rise immediately to the surface. Why is the CTN channel unprofitable? What can be done to change the ways of transacting business through these channels? Should the CTNs be made to buy through the wholesaler, rather than be serviced directly by the company's own salesforce?

The final study shows how an American building supplies company used ABC to evaluate the profitability of alternative distribution channels. This company had six distribution channels, four in the

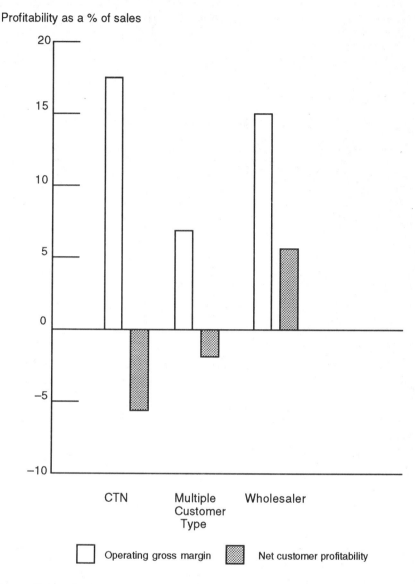

Figure 7.2 Comparison of gross and net profitability in the UK confectionery market

commercial market and two in the consumer market. Channel profitability figures under the traditional costing method are shown in Figure 7.3.

Managers were concerned about the low operating margins in the commercial sector (which averaged only 10 per cent), so they focused

($000s) Commercial	Contract	Industrial Suppliers	Government	OEM	Total
Annual Sales	79,434	25,110	422	9,200	114,166
Gross Margin	34%	41%	23%	27%	35%
Gross Profit	27,375	10,284	136	2,461	43,690
SG&A Allowance	19,746	6,242	105	2,287	31,814
Operating Profit	7,629	4,042	31	174	11,876
Operating Margin	10%	16%	7%	2%	10%

Figure 7.3   Profits by commercial distribution channel (traditional system)

their attention on sales, marketing and administration costs which, under the existing system, were allocated to each channel according to sales revenue (on the basis of 25 per cent of sales value). Both the OEM and government channels looked marginal and were prime candidates for elimination. But once costs were analysed by their activity causes, the picture looked quite different, as Figure 7.4 shows.

($000s) Commercial	Contract	Industrial Suppliers	Government	OEM	Total
Gross Profit	27,375	10,284	136	2,461	40,256
Selling Expenses	12,780	3,764	44	845	17,433
SG&A Allowance	6,740	2,131	36	781	9,688
Operating Profit	7,855	4,389	56	835	13,135
Operating Margin	10%	17%	13%	9%	12%

Figure 7.4   Profits by commercial distribution channel (activity-based system)

Because both the OEM and government channels used very few sales and marketing resources, the activity analysis showed their real profitability in a different light. The OEM channel showed a revised operating profit of 9 per cent (up from 2 per cent), which radically changed management's view of its future. Moreover, more realistic returns on investment in both the OEM and government channels were determined when the real capital resources used were correctly identified. With few inventories and low levels of receivables (and thus lower invested capital), the real returns in these channels were increased to 30 per cent compared with the 4 and 17 per cent calculated under the previous system.

If the figures in these examples have general validity, one might reasonably ask why companies do not perform more of this type of analysis and 'do something' about the large numbers of unprofitable customers. Some possible reasons come to mind. First, most information systems don't produce this type of analysis and therefore 'customer-specific' overheads are not identified; and secondly, as already mentioned, most managers may implicitly believe there is a large body of fixed costs which exist independently of the number of customers and, therefore, provided some contribution is made to these costs, most customers continue to be worthwhile.

In fact, such is the lack of progress in developing this type of analysis that a cynic might conclude that the main beneficiaries of this information (i.e. salespeople) don't actually want it. And it is not difficult to see why. Life would likely be more demanding if salespeople had to achieve targets on the basis of net profits. Many salespeople would only see tougher targets and declining rewards. So they have a vested interest in keeping as many customers as possible on the accounts receivable ledger. They even have their reasons for keeping customers whose continuing business might otherwise be questioned. How many times have you heard the following comments in response to a query regarding the profitability of particular customers?

❑ They are just about to place a big order.
❑ They are a good reference account.
❑ They are part of a bigger group and could be the key to dealing with other group companies.
❑ They buy the whole range of our products.

❑ We have dealt with them for more years than I can remember.
❑ We have spent a long time nurturing this account, we are not going to
   lose it now.
❑ From small acorns grow big oak trees.

Equally, developing customer profitability statements might detract from
the salespeople's ability to foist service-related costs on to other departments. Anderson and Narus allude to this in the following way: to close
a deal, a sales representative promises an extraordinary level of service
in the form of design assistance. Neither the customer nor the sales rep
is charged for the service. Instead, the charges are buried in the fixed
costs of the engineering department, which does the work for the
customer, making customer profitability difficult, if not impossible, to
measure.

The sales manager of a large American office equipment supplier had
this to say when asked about the profitability of his customers:

> It's management by anecdote. Salespeople regularly make passionate
> pleas for price relief on specific orders. When I press them for reasons,
> they say 'threat of competitive entry'. When I ask them if a cutback in
> service would be acceptable to make up for the price decrease, they give
> me a resounding no! What choice do you have in the absence of cost
> data, except to go by your judgment of the salesperson's credibility? I've
> wrongly accepted as many bad price relief requests as I've rejected.

As no two customers are the same, profitability can vary enormously.
Robin Bellis-Jones has pointed out that conventional accounting has
failed to recognise that the transaction is the common denominator
between product and customer and is therefore the ultimate profit centre.
He proposes an activity-based approach to measuring the costs of the
customer transaction based on the invoice line item. An activity-based
profit statement on the lines proposed by Bellis-Jones might appear as in
Figure 7.5.

Anderson and Narus point out that suppliers typically provide customers with more services than they want or need at prices that often
reflect neither the value of those services to customers nor the cost of

Revenue			xx
Less:	Cost of goods sold	x	
	Returned goods	x	
	Discounts and allowances	x	
Gross Margin			xx
Less:	Sales cost	x	
	Promotion cost (excluding media advertising	x	
	Product development cost	x	
	Direct warehousing cost	x	
	Customer transport cost	x	
	Post-sale service cost	x	
Net profit			xx

Figure 7.5   Sample activity-based customer profit statement

providing them. They suggest that ABC can be used to help firms match the cost of individual elements of customer service with the value provided for the customer. This 'value assessment' process has been successfully introduced at AKZO, the Dutch industrial coatings group.

Wondering whether the unit was providing more services than customers were paying for, managers developed ABC tools to analyse each customer's contribution to profits. Then they determined the value of each element of their service offering. As a result of the study, AKZO managers found that they were indeed providing more services than the customer was paying for, but, more importantly, they discovered that some of their services were of no value to customers. Armed with this information they were able to use customer-contribution-to-profit measures to revamp their services and prices, and target those industries and market segments with the greatest profit potential.

However, notwithstanding the efforts of ABC analysis, there appears to be a generalised and pervasive belief among many people that satisfying customer needs is the only worthwhile objective and that measurement systems, whether activity based or not, are irrelevant. Kaplan's view is as follows:

> I think that an unquestioned belief in meeting all customer needs and making all customers satisfied is demonstrably wrong. A customer based

ABC model can help managers decide when a customer's needs should not be satisfied, at least at the current price. Attempting to meet all customers' needs without regard to the economics of the customer transaction can lead a company not to the promised land of 'world class' performance, but to bankruptcy.

Most of the currently available evidence on customer profitability comes from activity-based studies. Although these highlight the extent of the problem, their results are, by definition, project based and piecemeal – criticisms repeatedly made throughout this book. And because they deal primarily with the better application of existing costs to customers, they don't provide managers with the help they need to determine which of these costs should be incurred in the first place. Thus customers are not only charged (rightly) with the costs which they consume, but also with the costs of irrelevant and poor quality work. If such costs could be separately analysed, the picture of customer, channel and market profitability might look very different – a point we argue in detail in Chapter 8. The evidence from the five ABC studies suggests that firms need new information systems to provide continuous data on customer profitability. We argue that such information can best be provided by a horizontal information system.

RETAINING PROFITABLE CUSTOMERS

How valuable to a company are customers over their lifetime? What is the loss of profit if they defect to the competition? Research has shown that, on average, a company can expect to lose 20 per cent of its customer base each year. This usually means that a large part of a company's sales effort goes into recruiting new customers to replace the ones they lose. Why do they allow this to happen and what can they do about it?

Studies by Bain & Co have shown that customers are more profitable the longer they remain with the company. After the initial marketing and set-up costs of acquiring customers have been incurred, customers begin to generate profits. Transactions become more straightforward –

customers become more familiar with the supplier's products, services, staff, and methods of working, thereby lowering costs for the supplier. Moreover, as the relationship matures, and as service, delivery and price expectations are fulfilled, customers increase their rate of repeat orders and, by relating their experience to others, bring new customers to the fold. And finally, once customers are accustomed to high levels of service, they become less sensitive to price, thus enabling margins to be improved (see Figure 7.6).

MBNA, the fast-growing US credit card company, is recognised to have one of the strongest reputations in its field for customer loyalty, and its results consistently bear this out. In the early 1980s the company announced its intention to improve customer satisfaction and to make every effort to keep all its customers. It made a number of changes to its performance measures and gathered information on customer defections. Now MBNA has one of the lowest defection rates in the industry and has

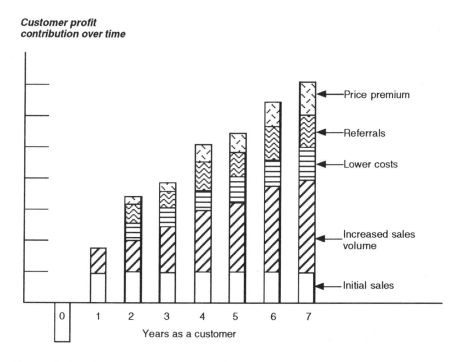

Figure 7.6   Customer profit contribution over time

increased its earnings dramatically. Between 1982 and 1990, for example, its industry ranking went from number 38 to 4, and its profits increased sixteenfold. Being the 'loyalty leader' in this market is now one of its primary objectives. Managers believe that customer loyalty pays big dividends and they now track 15 measures of customer satisfaction daily. The average balance of its cardholders is $2500 compared with the industry average of $1600 and its retention rate of profitable customers is up to 98 per cent.

If customers do defect, MBNA's first response is to try to win them back. The company has created a customer-defection 'swat' team filled with its best tele-marketers. This team is successful in winning lost customers back to the company 50 per cent of the time. But the company also gains valuable information from such defections and uses this to improve its levels of customer service. Unlike customer satisfaction surveys, such information is fresh, relevant and highly focused.

Another company that has taken the management of customer defections into the core of its strategy is American Express. According to one recent article:

> By the year end American Express intends to put an end to cold calling and to award planners [independent salespeople] bonuses for scoring well on customer satisfaction surveys. The goals of the redesign are explicit: a 95% client retention; 80% planner retention after 4 years; and an annual growth of 18%.

The management of defections also provides valuable information about the current performance of a company. But the reasons for defecting are often depressingly familiar – poor service from unconcerned and poorly trained employees.

THE SERVICE–PROFIT CHAIN

The strength of customer relationships, the quality of service and the satisfaction of employees are not measures which appear on corporate profit and loss statements, but their importance in evaluating performance is increasingly becoming recognised. There is a strong correlation between good service, profitability and employee satisfaction. This comment from a recent article captures the relationship well:

> The links in the chain are as follows: profit and growth are stimulated primarily by customer loyalty. Loyalty is a direct result of customer satisfaction. Satisfaction is largely influenced by the value of services provided to customers. Value is created by satisfied, loyal, and productive employees. Employee satisfaction in turn, results primarily from high-quality support services and policies that enable employees to deliver results to customers.

This 'service–profit chain' is illustrated in Figure 7.7 and discussed further below.

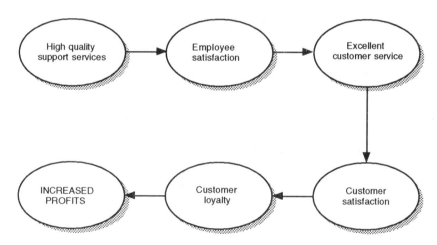

Figure 7.7   The service–profit chain

Customer loyalty drives profitability and growth

Reichheld and Sasser have suggested that when manufacturing companies started targeting 'zero defects' for their products, the quality revolution took off. In their view, zero defects is a target which is equally applicable to service companies. They explain that 'service companies have their own kind of scrap heap: customers who will not come back'. They argue that companies with loyal, long-term customers can financially outperform competitors with lower unit costs and high market share but a high turnover of customers. In their view the 'quality of market share, measured in terms of customer loyalty, deserves as much attention as quantity of share'.

One recent article discussed the 'real magic' of customer loyalty:

> Increase it, and a beneficial flywheel effect kicks in. Powered by repeat sales and referrals, revenue and market share grow. Costs fall because you don't exert excess energy foraging to replace defectors. Loyal customers expect a good price, but they crave value most of all. Rather than becoming an enemy, price then becomes a tool to filter out buyers who'll bolt for a penny. These steady customers are also easier to serve; they understand your modus operandi and make fewer demands on employee time. But when they ask, do come running. The payback? A Bain & Co study estimates that a decrease in the customer defection rate by 5 per cent can boost profits by 25 per cent to 95 per cent.

Honda, the Japanese car manufacturer, has improved its owner repurchase rate to 65 per cent compared with the industry average of 40 per cent. The company points to its simple and straightforward product line which makes it easier for its dealers to get to know and understand their customers.

The literature is full of examples of organisations which recognise (and quantify) the long-term benefits of customer loyalty. The Marriott hotel group, for example, reckons it adds $50 million to revenues for every one point increase in customer satisfaction ratings. The IBM plant in Minnesota has calculated that over a five-year period, a 1 per cent increase in customer satisfaction brings in a further $257 million in revenue. The owner of a Domino's Pizza franchise considers that each satisfied customer is worth $5000 over 10 years. Ford has also recognised the importance of retaining profitable customers:

> Dealers seem excited. The division has its new structure in place. It has defined comprehensive core processes. It has set bold stretch targets of

increasing customer retention – the percentage of Ford owners whose next car is also a Ford – from 60% to 80%. Each additional percentage point is worth a staggering $100 million in profits.

Customer satisfaction drives customer loyalty

Managers in service companies have difficulty measuring their operational performance because service quality, customer satisfaction and loyalty are rarely tracked by their accounting systems. Traditional accounting models assume that location strategies and sales promotions drive the top line and that the control of unit costs will bring bottom-line profits, but recent research is changing this perspective. For example, research on customer loyalty in the service sector has shown that only 14 per cent of customers stop buying from a business because of the poor quality of the product – but more than two-thirds defect because of inept or indifferent service. The hidden impact of poor service can be devastating. According to Robert Ayling, CEO of British Airways:

> The retention of customers can be briefly defined as: service delivery = zero defects; and service recovery = zero defections. Our statistics tell us that customers who experience bad service complain, on average, to 11 people, while those who experience good service tell only 6 people.

Many companies now conduct regular customer surveys and take action based on them. Xerox has gone further than most. It regularly contacts hundreds of thousands of customers per year and asks them to rank the company's products on a satisfaction scale from 0 to 5 (5 being the highest). In 1991 a more detailed analysis of purchasing habits of customers who gave Xerox scores of 4 and 5 on satisfaction found that customers giving 5s (i.e. very satisfied customers) were six times as likely to repurchase Xerox products as those who gave 4s (i.e. quite satisfied). These conclusions led to Xerox's descriptions of customers as 'apostles' – they were so delighted they persuaded their friends to buy from Xerox – and 'terrorists' (they were so dissatisfied they told their friends to have nothing to do with the company). Its current target is for 100 per cent of its customers to be 'apostles' by 1996.

Excellent service drives customer satisfaction

Arthur D Little has discovered a basic truth concerning service quality, one that is found in every industry it has studied: improved service quality results in a consistent pattern of increased market share and revenues. In the case of a large sportswear manufacturer managers saw an opportunity to increase its 10 per cent market share by improving critical areas of service. It did this by finding out where its two main rivals, who owned 60 per cent of the market between them, were falling down. These failings turned out to be a mixture of product attributes (breadth, style, and quality), service attributes (order fill, delivery, order accuracy, responsiveness to emergencies, and problem-solving capabilities) and value attributes (reasonable payment terms). By concentrating on improving these aspects of customer value the company increased its market share by 2 per cent and its revenues by 20 per cent.

ADL believes the relationship between service and price is even more direct. In the case of a plastic laminates manufacturer it calculated that out of 25 categories, 9 had a major impact on price. Figure 7.8 shows the different elements of the service package and how the impact each has on the extra price which can be commanded. According to ADL, customers were prepared to pay an aggregate 7 per cent price premium for the value of these extra services. And what's more, it suggests that this rule is applicable in most industries.

Data collected by the US Department of Consumer Affairs provides further evidence. It shows that when customers experience minor problems, 95 per cent say they will repurchase if the complaint is resolved quickly, but if the complaint takes a little longer to be resolved this figure drops to 70 per cent. The effect of speedy problem resolution illustrates the difference between excellent and poor performance at the operating level.

	% Price increase
Product attributes	
Product line scope	1.4
Consistent quality	0.4
Finishing capabilities	0.2
Service attributes	
Accuracy of shipment to order	2.4
Carrier capability	0.8
Handling of rush orders	0.6
Problem-solving helpfulness	0.4
Notification when shipment is delayed	0.2
Value attributes	
Reasonable payment terms	0.6
TOTAL PRICE IMPACT	7.0

Figure 7.8   The price premium from extra services

Employee satisfaction drives excellent service

Employee satisfaction is the central ingredient in understanding the relationship between customer service and profitability. This has much to do with the 'feelgood factor'. Most employees feel good if they deal with customers who are happy with the service they receive. Banc One Corporation, for example, has developed a sophisticated system to track several indices of customer loyalty and satisfaction. Once driven strictly by financial measures, the bank now conducts quarterly measures of customer retention; the number of services used by each customer, or depth of relationship; and the level of customer satisfaction. The strategies derived from this information help explain why Banc One has achieved a return on assets more than double that of its competitors in recent years and has grown faster than most of its rivals.

Further evidence is provided by the experience of an American property-and-casualty insurance company. A 1991 study not only identified the links between employee satisfaction and loyalty, but also established that a primary source of job satisfaction was the service workers' perception of their ability to meet customer needs. Those who felt they did meet customer needs registered levels more than twice as high as those who felt they didn't. But even more importantly, the same study found that when a service worker left the company, customer satisfaction levels dropped sharply from 75 to 55 per cent. As a result of this analysis, managers are trying to reduce turnover among customer-contact employees and to enhance their job skills.

Traditional methods of measuring the costs of employee turnover focus on recruitment and training. They ignore the much larger (but mainly invisible) costs of a decline in employee productivity and decreased customer satisfaction. One securities broker reckoned it takes five years to rebuild relationships with customers that can return $1 million per year in commissions – a cumulative loss of $2.5 million in commission income.

The increasing use of technology can (paradoxically) be a negative factor in the customer service link. Inflexible computer systems often cannot handle a small variation in an order, and computer systems intended for direct customer use frequently do not work. Customers want to be made to feel comfortable, not put under pressure. To visit a bank, retail store or hotel and be met with a friendly familiar face is (literally) worth its weight in gold. The influence of technology is particularly insidious when managers mistakenly believe that technology supports employee empowerment. But according to Schlesinger and Heskett:

> The growing body of data we have collected thus far suggests that customer satisfaction is rooted in employee satisfaction and retention more than in anything else, including clever technology (especially clever technology, since competitors can so easily replicate it). To go one step further, if the technology restricts employee latitude and perhaps even customer choice, as is the case in some of the businesses we have observed, it can actually create a constraint on strategic alternatives and long-term performance.

While many organisations are beginning to recognise the links in the service–profit chain, few have taken the step of linking this with strategy. One exception is Taco Bell, the fast food subsidiary of Pepsico. Taco Bell's management tracks profits daily by unit, market manager, zone and country. By linking this information with exit interviews covering 800,000 customers annually, the company has found that stores in the top quadrant of customer satisfaction ratings outperform the others on all measures. As a result it has linked no less than 20 per cent of all operating managers' compensation to customer satisfaction ratings.

By examining employee turnover records for individual stores, the company discovered that the 20 per cent of stores with the lowest turnover rates were also the highest performers in terms of sales and profits. Sales were doubled and profits were 55 per cent higher than in those stores with the highest employee turnover rate. Taco Bell has now implemented employee satisfaction programmes which involve better selection procedures, improved skill building, increased latitude for on-the-job decision making, further automation of 'unpleasant' back-room tasks, and greater promotional opportunities.

High quality service drives employee satisfaction

The quality of the working environment contributes most to employee satisfaction. How employees feel about their jobs, colleagues and companies are the primary determinants of satisfied employees. As discussed above, research has shown that service employees value their ability and authority to achieve results for customers higher than anything else.

The Ritz-Carlton Hotel Co takes customer service further than most. The company has given employees the flexibility to spend up to $2000 to resolve a customer problem – however long it takes – and employees can break off from their current task to deal with the customer. The results of this policy are that more than 90 per cent of Ritz-Carlton's customers return, and the rate is even higher for customers who hold meetings in the hotels.

8

IMPLEMENT A HORIZONTAL
INFORMATION SYSTEM

Management accountants need to change their focus in designing their systems from an information-for-decisions to a behaviour-influencing focus...the primary concern of the behaviour-influencing approach is to design a system to influence employees to do the desired things.

Toshiro Hiromoto

IMAGINE FOR A MOMENT THAT YOU ARE CHIEF EXECUTIVE OF A LARGE organisation. But this organisation is different – its old vertical management structures and information systems have been turned on their side and now face horizontally towards the customer. With the data stream flowing laterally across the company (following the chain of value-adding work), systems can now report on the *net profits* of distribution channels, products and customers; identify where work adds value; report on the efficiency of processes; and say whether strategic targets are being achieved. And what's more, managers can take decisions that clearly relate to these targets (indeed, they are rewarded for doing so).

If such reports can be generated, surely no self-respecting manager would be without them? So why haven't they already been widely implemented? Is it because they are seen to be impractical? Billions of dollars are incurred every year on the development and maintenance of accounting systems which, by and large, simply reinforce the hierarchical structure. Although activity-based systems are becoming more common, we have argued that such approaches fail to report systematically on non-value-adding work, and thus don't provide managers with the means to eliminate it. Activity-based studies reveal that the cost of such unnecessary work is far higher than most managers imagine, and that the benefits to the bottom line of its removal are potentially huge.

Again, if the removal of this work offers such rewards, why haven't firms introduced systems to track and analyse it? The probable answer is that the success of horizontal systems relies extensively on worker participation and information sharing, the very notions of which are alien to most organisations. So proposals to move in this direction are easy prey to cynical managers who cast doubt that such participation is feasible. Other reasons come to mind. For example, finance managers are notoriously conservative, and any new ideas which appear to impinge on their ability to produce traditional numbers quickly are likely to be given short shrift. Moreover, the investment cost of new systems and the extent of the disruption to the smooth running of existing systems can be exaggerated. Lack of managerial understanding concerning the extent of non-value-adding costs may also be a contributing factor. Because executives and managers are not confronted with the size of the problem (it is not information required by accounting bodies and does not need to be placed on public view), the issue is often brushed aside. This is a serious misconception. Here is Kaplan on the topic:

> I just can't believe that any organisation would be unwilling to incur this cost [of new systems] given that only 20 per cent of its products may be making money, or only 20 per cent of its customers may be profitable...the value of the insights you get from understanding much more accurately what causes your operating expenses and where your profits are being earned just overwhelms the implementation costs of these systems. The real cost is the cost of education, of overcoming organisational resistance, of changing the way we've approached the subject the last thirty or forty years.

But the issue which concerns us most is not cost or disruption, but feasibility. Horizontal systems *are* difficult to implement within a traditional structure. They are designed primarily to fit horizontal structures. And their success depends on the support of the workforce. This is the nub of the matter. The question then becomes whether it is practical to train workers to understand which aspects of their work add value, and whether they can be relied on to report honestly when they are performing non-value-adding work. If this can be achieved, software designers can do the rest.

We believe it can be achieved. We have noted that Japanese workers report wasted work and that American workers at NUMMI, Kodak, Lincoln Electric, Hewlett-Packard and GE are already several steps down this path. Generating a clear list of activities for each worker is the starting point. Introducing horizontal systems as a shared information framework rather than as a control mechanism is a precondition of acceptance and future commitment.

We believe that horizontal systems will develop rapidly once designers put their minds to the task. Modern computer systems now have the power and flexibility to cope with the challenge. It took many years and countless versions of hardware and software before existing general ledger analysis reached its current level of analytical detail. The same evolution can be expected with horizontal systems, but compacted within a much shorter time frame. We recognise that designing and implementing horizontal systems will not be easy. The attributes required are faith, determination and lateral thinking. This chapter offers some guidance by following the progress of a hypothetical company, Virtual Computers Limited (VCL), as it transforms its performance through the implementation of a horizontal information system.

VIRTUAL COMPUTERS LIMITED: A CASE FOR TRANSFORMATION

VCL manufactures powerful computer workstations, file servers and desktop PCs, and provides a range of services such as consultancy, maintenance and training. The results for last year showed that sales were $1.2 billion and that a net loss was incurred of $5 million, compared with a profit of $50 million the year before and $80 million the year before that. The current year suggested little sign of recovery, so the directors decided to hire a new CEO, Dick Davis, a turnaround specialist. Three years later turnover was up to $2.5 billion and profits were $350 million. How was this transformation achieved?

Asking the right questions

We begin with a series of meetings between Dick Davis and his management team which reveal many of the problems confronting the business. Dick's first meeting is with the chairman, Bill Burgess, an experienced businessman with a successful track record. Bill was finding it difficult to explain the recent setbacks at VCL. He was a tough no-nonsense negotiator who believed in working hard and playing hard, and expected total commitment from his staff. Dick Davis opened the meeting.

CEO: Bill, I'm anxious to know about the company's financial position, its strategy, and the state of the market.

CHAIRMAN: Well Dick, I have to tell you that the situation is pretty bad. In fact, we're in grave danger of breaching our banking covenants, and our major shareholders are demanding more action.

CEO: Tell me what action you've already taken.

CHAIRMAN: I think the right question might be what action haven't we taken. We've tried just about everything. In fact some people in the firm think that our consultants have taken up residence. We've instigated over 20 quality programmes, many reengineering projects, and we've moved to just-in-time production. We've also cut costs, product lines, prices, and over a thousand jobs. And we've reduced our overheads by 15 per cent over the past 18 months.

CEO: What happened then?

CHAIRMAN: Results improved for about six months but then the losses reappeared – we were devastated. It seems that we lost many of our larger customers, followed by some of our best salespeople.

CEO: Was this a coincidence?

CHAIRMAN: I doubt it. There's been a lot of bad feeling in the firm over the cuts. In fact we've also lost quite a few of our best researchers and engineers – some of whom had been with us for years.

CEO: Tell me about your strategy.

CHAIRMAN: Well, a major plank in our strategy is to continue to improve the technical features of our products and make it more difficult for the competition to catch us. In this way we can get better prices and margins and keep our customers locked in. Protecting our customers is central to our whole approach.

CEO: Is this working?

CHAIRMAN: I think so, although I must say that some of our competitors also have good products. The bad news is that they've been undercutting us on price. Dick, I'm bound to say that talking about strategy is fine in theory, but what really counts is achieving this quarter's budget.

CEO: Can you describe the management structure?

CHAIRMAN: Sure. We have clear lines of authority throughout our functions and departments. We also operate a form of 'matrix management' where, for example, technical support engineers across the firm report both to their local managers and to their functional superiors at head office. This system has been developed over many years and everyone understands it. There is a clear promotion path for all our employees to follow from apprentice to chief executive. We also have reward systems to support this structure.

CEO: Tell me more about these reward systems.

CHAIRMAN: These haven't changed for years. Our production people are rewarded according to volume-related bonuses; our sales people are rewarded against quota and gross profit targets; and our managers are rewarded according to divisional profits. Oh, let's not forget our top executives who are rewarded according to group profits and earnings per share. But of course all this is academic as no one has had any bonuses for over 12 months.

Dick's next meeting was with the finance director, John Kelly. John was proud of his systems and how quickly they could generate information, but Dick was more interested in the relevance of the information than its speed of production.

CEO: John, I'm interested to know more about your information systems and how you measure performance.

FINANCE DIRECTOR: Look Dick, whatever we say about systems and performance, the only performance that matters to shareholders and bankers is this quarter's results. I know we should be taking a longer term view, but if survival depends on the support of the banks – and it does – we need to satisfy them first, it's a simple fact of business life.

CEO: Listen John, I'm not trying out some new kind of business theory here. I also understand the real world – the problem is that we're not living in it. Now let's start with the marketplace. Why do customers buy from us and not from the competition?

FINANCE DIRECTOR: Our customer surveys show that they care most about quality, service, product reliability, the frequency of new products, and of course, price.

CEO: Now tell me how we measure performance.

FINANCE DIRECTOR: That's not so easy because we prepare an information package for different management levels within the business.

CEO: Just describe those reports.

FINANCE DIRECTOR: Well, our monthly reporting system includes profits by division and department, growth in sales, gross profits, return on sales, return on net assets, and earnings per share. And all these are of course compared rigorously against budget. We also produce cost and efficiency variances to control product costs, and use marginal costing to ensure that all products make a worthwhile contribution to overheads.

CEO: What's the purpose of these reports?

FINANCE DIRECTOR: They give us real control over costs and capital spending. Our budgeting systems are detailed and very comprehensive – without them we would be in a much bigger mess.

CEO: But what relevance do these reports have to the key competitive issues you mentioned a few moments ago?

FINANCE DIRECTOR: I don't follow your point. Our systems are designed to produce information for management decisions, and our priority is to do this as fast as possible so that immediate action can be taken if things go wrong.

CEO: But doesn't it seem crazy to you that we don't measure the most important factors that determine our future well-being – the very factors you said only a few moments ago were critical to our success, quality, service, speed, and so on – factors which affect customers and lead directly to their future buying decisions? What sort of management behaviour do you think your reporting systems encourage?

FINANCE DIRECTOR: Good housekeeping and attention to detail. All costs are scrutinised carefully – we really run a tight ship. Our objective every month is to maximise profits throughout the organisation.

The next meeting on Dick Davis's agenda was with the quality manager, Bert Young, who had only been with the firm a few years but was totally frustrated with its inability to take quality seriously. Dick Davis opened the discussion.

CEO: Bert, quality in all its guises is central to my whole approach, so I need to know how we measure it, and how effective our programmes are.

QUALITY MANAGER: Well, we've been operating quality programmes for the past five years, and although we've achieved some progress, it's nowhere near as good as I'd hoped.

CEO: What support do you get from top management?

QUALITY MANAGER: Not enough. They know that we need to improve quality but they look on us as a cost rather than a profit centre.

CEO: Why's that?

QUALITY MANAGER: Probably because they can't see how we directly benefit the bottom line.

CEO: How would you address that problem?

QUALITY MANAGER: Everybody here knows that our quality is poor compared with some of our major competitors. They also don't need much convincing that the real costs of poor quality are huge. But because we can't measure it more precisely – who can? – they prefer to ignore it, or more accurately, pay lip-service to it.

CEO: Have you ever heard of a 'work audit'?

QUALITY MANAGER: No, why do you ask?

CEO: Some companies have used consultants who specialise in analysing people's work and evaluating whether it's of benefit to the customer. In fact it's not uncommon for these reports to show that the majority of all work adds no value at all.

QUALITY MANAGER: That doesn't surprise me. I would certainly welcome that sort of initiative here. Anything that raises the profile of quality and productivity in this place will get my whole-hearted support.

Dick's final meeting was with Will Barnes, the IT manager.

CEO: Will, I'm interested to know what software you have and what information you produce.

IT MANAGER: Our systems are fairly standard – we have financial systems and manufacturing and distribution packages which were specially written for our requirements. Our finance people seem quite happy that we can produce their accounts within a few days of the period end – that's all that seems to matter.

CEO: What information do you produce for the finance people?

IT MANAGER: They receive incredible levels of cost analysis by every segment of the business. Every motor vehicle has its own cost account. We also have a very comprehensive budgeting system which gives them lots of control. In fact the last major update to the system included even more detailed analysis within the general ledger, as well as an executive information system which summarises key data for top management.

CEO: What kind of data?

IT MANAGER: Oh, sales and gross profit by product, area, market, etc., sales per employee, actual versus budget in all departments – that type of information. We've recently added some operating statistics such as on-time delivery, and time to market, but we have to use PCs to gather it together – it takes quite a bit of time.

CEO: Has anyone ever suggested that we measure the net profitability of products and customers?

IT MANAGER: Not to my knowledge. How would we do that anyway?

Dick Davis reflected on his various meetings. VCL was in even worse shape than he imagined. Managers were acting as if the company existed in a vacuum protected from customers and competitors alike. The only saving grace was evidence of good products and a bunch of engineers with lots of flair, but with no sense of cost. He was also optimistic that some managers could begin to perform well if they were given a clear sense of direction.

After recruiting a new finance director and a new IT manager, Dick was ready to begin the job in earnest. Strategy was the first issue to sort out, and agreement was soon reached that the primary objective was to become a major world player in the 'power-server' market and build a solid reputation for client-server systems. To achieve this the company would have to rebuild customer relationships, streamline costs, and improve production scheduling, quality and efficiency. But above all they needed to restructure the business along process lines, focus on attaining customer and strategic targets, and cut out work which added no value.

After a series of meetings and visits to other organisations, the management team decided to reorganise the business into six key processes:

① Research and development, including new product design, development and prototyping
② Order generation, including marketing, sales, order processing and accounts receivable
③ Procurement, including purchase ordering, inventory management and accounts payable
④ Manufacturing, including bills of material, production, final assembly and despatch
⑤ Service, incorporating all aspects of after-sales service including maintenance and user support
⑥ Education, training and consultancy

But Dick Davis knew from previous experience that measuring and encouraging the right value-adding work is the real key to long-term success. And he had set that challenge to his new finance and IT managers.

The causes of costs

Before Dick Davis could set about developing new systems, he had to convince the management team that the real problems lay with the high levels of non-value-adding work. To do this he commissioned two consulting reports, one a work audit, and the other concerned with the performance of a sales region. The report on the work audit confirmed Dick Davis's worst fears – the level of non-value-adding work was between 10 and 15 per cent of sales (between $120 million and $180 million per year).

These figures shocked the management team, although some remained sceptical. But the report on the sales region, which was the more specific, would finally convince them. A meeting was arranged for Dick Davis, Bill Burgess and the consultant Don Goodman to meet the sales director, Tim Rhodes, and the manager of the sales area which was chosen for the study, Harry Mitchell. We pick up the discussion between sales director and sales manager before the others arrive.

SALES DIRECTOR: Harry, I thought we might just have a few words together before we hear what Don Goodman has to say. These expenses for last year – you've done pretty well – I see you've kept your costs nicely under budget. I wish I could say the same for a number of other regions.

SALES MANAGER: Thanks Tim. It wasn't easy, but we managed to finally show a favourable variance of $300,000 against budget. I must say the accounting department's detailed reports have helped a lot. My salespeople now control their budgets very closely. I think the message has really sunk in.

SALES DIRECTOR: Do you think you can do better this year? What's your budgeted expenditure?

SALES MANAGER: Well, conditions out there aren't likely to improve much next year. We'll be lucky to hit the same level of sales as this year, but we're still shooting for a 5 per cent cost reduction. So our final budget is $6,175,000.

SALES DIRECTOR: How did you get to the final figure?

SALES MANAGER: Well, we looked in detail at all the various cost categories that the accountants give us. It was hard to cut salaries and benefits – though we've managed a little bit here and there and cut two salespeople – so most of the projected savings will come from even tighter control of travelling, telephone, and a number of other small items.

With the preliminaries over, Tim invited Dick Davis, Bill Burgess and Don Goodman to join the meeting. Tim turned to Don:

SALES DIRECTOR: So, tell us Don, what have we been doing wrong?

CONSULTANT: Well, if you remember Tim, my terms of reference included an assessment of the effectiveness of the sales force – and so I began by asking some fairly basic questions, to give myself a clearer picture of the issues involved. My questions included: Why do we have a sales force at all? What do the salespeople actually do? How do they spend their time? And in particular, how much time do they spend in front of customers? Do the customers like the salespeople? You might be surprised to know that the answers to these simple questions weren't easy to find.

SALES DIRECTOR: Well I wouldn't have thought it mattered that much provided we hit our targets, but please carry on.

CONSULTANT: We gather lots of detail on how much is spent on making phone calls, entertaining clients and travelling to customers, but not much on the time the salespeople spend on doing what they are (presumably) paid to do. Anyway, as a result of our brief analysis, we've come up with some initial data which we'd like to show you. Even at this stage there are a few surprises.

SALES DIRECTOR: Such as?

CONSULTANT: Let's begin with the existing budgeting system. Looking at last year's figures, the picture is fairly clear. The sales department's costs are less than expected. *(turns to the flipchart)*

Sales Cost Budget ($000s)

Financial Costs	Budget	Actual	Variance
Salaries	4100	4000	100
Benefits	400	400	–
Travelling	800	700	100
Car	350	300	50
Occupancy	300	300	–
Telephone	850	800	50
TOTALS	6800	6500	300

Activity Costs		
Visiting customers	1400
Travelling	1200
Processing orders	300
Reprocessing orders	400
Checking prices	800
Chasing factory	800
Attending meetings	1600
TOTALS	6500

CONSULTANT: From the top half of the flipchart, you can see that $300,000 has been 'saved'. But if we look through a different lens at the actual work of the salespeople, and how this work translates into activity costs, we see a completely different picture. What do these figures tell you?

SALES DIRECTOR: I must confess that I've never thought of the business in this way before. If I interpret these figures correctly, the work which makes any difference to customers is only represented by the first three headings – and that's only just over half the total cost! That means the salespeople are spending the majority of their time on work which adds no value for the customer.

SALES MANAGER: Like you Tim, my first reaction is one of surprise. I was aware that my people frequently complained about problems caused by other departments, but I'd no idea of the extent of the time they spent solving them. And the accountant's reports certainly don't deal with these questions.

SALES DIRECTOR: I need some time to think about all this Don, but one of my first reactions is that we seem to expect our customers to pay for a hell of a lot of inefficiencies.

CONSULTANT: But that's exactly the point, Tim. Let's look at the question another way. The salespeople are the last link in the chain of activities which ends up with the customer. They must be sure all the problems are solved prior to delivery, otherwise they will again be on the wrong end of the customer's tongue. So what do they do? They chase the factory if it doesn't keep its delivery promises, they check prices because the price list is out of date or prone to errors, they attend meetings to solve a multitude of small problems, and they spend hours on the phone placating customers with a creative list of excuses which try to give the impression that most problems are not of their own making. The frustration from the salesperson's point of view is that most of the problems are caused elsewhere, although I have to say that they're not blameless themselves. You only have to look at how many orders they get right first time to realise this – it's pretty low.

SALES DIRECTOR: Hell Don, just think what our salespeople could do with their time if they weren't tied up solving all these problems. We could put them in front of more customers more of the time. Imagine what that would do to productivity! Incidentally, are these good profitable customers?

CONSULTANT: Good question. I said at the beginning that this was very much a first report. But the answer is no, we're not sure if all customers are profitable. Indeed the salespeople are not that concerned either, because you reward them on the basis of gross revenue rather than profitability. We have to do a lot more work in this area, but my guess is that salespeople spend a disproportionate amount of time with a small number of very awkward customers who demand the earth and often get it. We could very well find that some of these are unprofitable.

SALES DIRECTOR: Well, I can see how this can improve our budgeting and how it can help us manage work, but how on earth are we going to measure it? Surely without such a system, all these great ideas will come to nothing?

CEO: You can see what we're talking about more clearly when you look at next year's sales expense budget. Sure, we've budgeted for a 5 per cent cost reduction. And so have many other departments. Everybody realises the importance of reducing costs. But it's now clear that reducing costs is the wrong emphasis. We should be reducing, and indeed eliminating, the work we don't need to do. But that's hard to achieve, because we don't ask the right questions. So we get a sales budget of $6,175,000, whereas it's quite possible that the salespeople could make even more dramatic reductions if they could just stop doing all this stuff which adds no value for anyone. You think the budget reduction looks good, but in reality we are still building all the non-value-adding work into next year's target. This means that we might well reach our cost reduction targets, but we'll find we're placing the same workload on fewer shoulders – and then more and more people will get disillusioned with 70-hour weeks. We have to cut the workload, not the workforce.

Dick knew that Bill Burgess was convinced by listening to this discussion. A number of similar meetings followed. Dick saw budgeting as the ideal way to get across the basic concept of how work drives costs. However, he also knew that people would soon revert to their old ways of thinking unless he could create new methods of systematically measuring it.

Implementing a horizontal information system

A special team was set up to design and develop the new 'horizontal' system. But when Dick Davis met the IT manager, Jo Hill, he wasn't aware that she was so far down the line.

CEO: How's the new system coming along, Jo?

IT MANAGER: It's taken longer than we expected to complete the new software, but we're now happy that it runs well, and doesn't impose any additional processing overhead on our existing financial systems. Our systems designers have done an excellent job of integrating the old and new systems while maintaining integrity and security where it matters.

CEO: How did you get on with the activity analysis?

IT MANAGER: Don Goodman helped us here. By the way, the various discussions we had about activity analysis produced lots of new ideas on how we could improve customer value. It made us look at our processes in a very different way. Take the procurement process, for example. We now have integrated purchasing, inventory management and accounts payable. This means that one process can deal with all the issues arising within this area of the business. Problems are now being solved much more quickly than before, but more importantly, the problems are disappearing.

CEO: What difficulties have you encountered?

IT MANAGER: Once we'd completed the activity analysis we spent a lot of time discussing how relevant each activity is to customers. Even with Don's help it was difficult to get people to accept some of the activity ratings which were finally agreed on.

CEO: What do you mean by 'activity ratings'?

IT MANAGER: We start with the principle that people's work can be broken down into activities, and that each activity can be measured according to its relevance or the value it provides for the customer.

We then separate primary activities, which add value for customers, from secondary activities, which don't directly add value, but are nevertheless necessary to enable primary activities to take place. By the way, that's the easy part, although even this has thrown up some surprises. We start by looking at each activity in two ways. First we put on the 'activity hat' and argue the merits of the activity against its objective, which of course is usually satisfying the customer. Then we put on the 'customer hat' and discuss the worth of the activity from the customer's point of view. This method enables us to look at the issue from both angles without the petty squabbles which would no doubt happen if we turned the meeting into a debating chamber.

CEO: What's so important about these ratings?

IT MANAGER: They're important because they define the worth of an activity to what I would call in computing terms a 'reporting category', such as the customer. Our primary objective is to continuously improve the worth of our activities and the ratings system focuses the time of our people on those activities that add the most value. We are aware that this is open to some abuse, but with the main targets set by process teams, there is terrific pressure on the teams to improve their overall performance. We've already seen examples where team members have told their colleagues to improve their performance, otherwise they won't survive.

CEO: Isn't it all a bit subjective?

IT MANAGER: It will be to start with, but in the early phase of development these ratings are only meant to provide a starting point for the measurement system. Whether internal training, for example, is rated at 25 or 50 per cent is not the point, nor is the overall index being 77.2 or 59.8 per cent. The real issue is how we can make improvements in the index from the baseline we start with, and this is more concerned with the reorganisation of work than with individual ratings. For example, we want to encourage more work to be of the primary category than the secondary category. In any case, the 'quality of work' is probably more important than its relevance.

CEO: How do you deal with the issue of quality?

IT MANAGER: Our quality index measures that aspect of work which is performed correctly first time. In other words, by measuring the cost of people doing things they shouldn't be doing in the first place, usually because someone else has made a mess of it, we can see the net value of the good work they do.

CEO: What do you see as the main benefit of this system?

IT MANAGER: We've developed the idea of a new type of productivity index which we think deals with the contribution of non-manual workers much better than before. We've called it a 'value-adding work index' or VAWI, and it measures the proportion of work which truly adds value for the customer. We believe that this will enable managers to measure people's real output and help them budget for their time. The implications for salespeople, designers, engineers and everyone in process teams are quite far-reaching.

CEO: Have you generated any reports yet?

IT MANAGER: As a matter of fact we have, although they're a bit rough at the edges. We could start by looking at the activity analysis for one of our key processes – procurement. This list shows the various activities:

1 Receive purchase orders from factory
2 Process purchase orders
3 Agree terms with suppliers
4 Set up new suppliers
5 Update parts list
6 Receive parts
7 Process goods received notes
8 Update inventory
9 Issue parts
10 Process purchase invoices
11 Deal with invoice queries
12 Process supplier payments

IT MANAGER: We also have to deal with shared overheads. The procurement team shares a building with manufacturing. The size of the building is 60,000 sq ft of which procurement occupies 12,000 sq ft. The ratio of other costs for manufacturing and procurement is facilities (rent and building costs) 90/10, utilities (energy costs) 95/5, and technology 60/40. It was also agreed that procurement absorbed an average of 25 per cent of all the costs of the specialist functions in the period. Our first objective was to re-analyse the general ledger costs to the activity ledger. This required a new coding system which we've designed. Again, let's look at the procurement part of the system. The balances at the end of period 1 in the general ledger are shown in this report here.

VCL Limited Period 1 Procurement Process General Ledger Balances	Total Cost (000s)	Analysed to A/L by
Salaries	75.0	Staff time
Wages & benefits	750.0	Staff time
Training	50.0	Staff time
Travelling	200.0	Staff time
Telephone	60.0	Staff time
General & admin expenses	150.0	Staff time
Occupancy (20%)	75.0	Tracing
Utilities (5%)	60.0	Tracing
Technology (40%)	90.0	Tracing
Specialist functions (25%)	240.0	Tracing
TOTAL	1750.0	

IT MANAGER: These balances include the share of costs applicable to the procurement process for the use of buildings, energy, technology and specialist functions. Group costs and interest have not been applied (we decided this would not be helpful in measuring process performance). The column on the right shows the basis on which we've analysed these costs to the new activity ledger. For example, salaries and travelling have been analysed by time spent, and functional costs by a method of 'tracing', that is, allocating them to each process by their use of these resources.

CEO: An activity ledger is a new one on me. What's it for?

IT MANAGER: First let me show you our main report which records the activity ledger balances and shows a full picture of process performance.

VCL Limited Procurement Process Activity Ledger Balances ($000s)	Total Cost	Costs of Poor Quality	Costs of Irrelevance	Net VA Work	Quality Index	Relevance Index	VAWI
Receive POs from factory	20.0	5.0	0	15.0	75.0%	100%	75.0%
Process purchase orders	120.0	30.0	0	90.0	75.0%	100%	75.0%
Agree terms with suppliers	60.0	0	0	60.0	100.0%	100%	100.0%
Set up new suppliers	40.0	0	0	40.0	100.0%	100%	100.0%
Update parts list	60.0	10.0	0	50.0	83.3%	100%	83.3%
Receive parts	20.0	10.0	0	10.0	50.0%	100%	50.0%
Process goods received note	150.0	50.0	0	100.0	66.7%	100%	66.7%
Update inventory	80.0	30.0	0	50.0	62.5%	100%	62.5%
Issue parts	60.0	33.0	0	27.0	45.0%	100%	45.0%
Process purchase invoices	180.0	60.0	0	120.0	66.7%	100%	66.7%
Deal with invoice queries	120.0	0	90.0	30.0	100.0%	25%	25.0%
Update supplier records	50.0	10.0	0	40.0	80.0%	100%	80.0%
Process management	200.0		50.0	150.0	100.0%	75%	75.0%
Attending meetings	75.0		56.0	18.8	100.0%	25%	25.0%
Training	50.0		12.5	37.5	100.0%	75%	75.0%
Occupancy	75.0		0	75.0	100.0%	100%	100.0%
Utilities	60.0		0	60.0	100.0%	100%	100.0%
Technology	90.0		0	90.0	100.0%	100%	100.0%
Specialist functions	240.0		60.0	180.0	100.0%	75%	75.0%
TOTAL	1750.0	238.0	268.5	1243.3	86.4%	86%	71.0%

IT MANAGER: If you look at the total, you will see that the $1.75 million of costs shown in the general ledger report now looks quite different. The same 'costs' have now been translated into the real work that people do – into their 'activities'. You can see that the extra quality costs have now been included. They amount to $238,000 in period 1. If we take the 'process goods received notes' activity, for example, we can see that $50,000 of non-value-adding costs (costs of poor quality) have been incurred out of the total activity cost of $150,000. In our new vocabulary, that means that its quality index is 66.7%, that is, two-thirds of the activity was performed well. Our other key measure is the 'value-adding work index' which is the net balance of an activity cost which is of value to a customer. Our overall objective is to maximise this value.

CEO: Jo, I think the message is getting through. The relevance index is 86%, the quality index is 86.4%, and the overall value-adding-work index is 71%. If my maths are correct, this means that 29% of procurement costs in period 1 – over $500,000 – were of no benefit to the customer. That represents a huge opportunity for improving profits. How accurate is this information?

IT MANAGER: Well, as I said earlier it's not yet as accurate as I would like, but real enough to cause alarm bells ringing around the organisation. Managers know that they will shortly be measured on this new system, and they are instigating all sorts of projects to increase their value-adding-work index. We also produce 'exception reports' which tell us the source of many of the problems. Much of this information comes from employee time records. We rely on employees recording any time spent on activities other than their own 'core' activities, and once they have realised the problem-solving capability of this information, they have responded remarkably well. For example, if a person processing purchase invoices can't find a matching purchase order, and they have to spend time investigating the problem, we want to know why this happened, who caused the problem, and how long it took to resolve. In this way we can not only start to identify the problems, but we can also take corrective action. All process teams will begin to understand this important discipline – the last thing they will want is to carry the can for someone else's mistakes or shoddy work. If we look at this report showing the total non-value-adding costs within the goods received area, we can now see how these costs were caused.

VCL Limited Period 1 Procurement Process Non-value-adding Costs of Goods Received Notes	Total Cost (000s)	Source of Problem
Wrong parts ordered	10.0	Factory
GRN & PO do not agree	20.0	Factory/Supplier
GRN not signed	3.0	Goods Received
Part shipment problem	6.0	Supplier
Goods not in a fit state	6.0	Supplier
Others	5.0	
TOTAL	50.0	

IT MANAGER: We've already started a number of investigations. For example, you can see that one of our main problems is that purchase invoices do not agree with purchase orders. We discussed this problem at length and decided to approach our top suppliers with the following proposition. We told them that unless their deliveries match our purchase orders exactly we will not accept them, but if the match is a good one, we will pay their invoices in 25 days instead of 30 days.

CEO: Well, I must say you're quick off the mark. Does this mean that we simply turn suppliers trucks around if they arrive with part orders or with one small defective part, or even a wrong part number?

IT MANAGER: Too right we do. Our suppliers don't argue any more. They know that the onus is on them to improve their systems or lose the business. But, although we don't yet have the final reports for period two, I can tell you that our costs in this area have dried up. That's just one example of the new questions that this type of system is prompting from our people. They want to improve things all the time. In fact, we have to hold them back, and insist that we take our time.

Like a scientist on the verge of a new discovery, Dick Davis was excited but cautious. He knew that the horizontal information system was the key to long-term value-adding performance, but these new systems needed more testing, and his managers needed convincing that these ideas could be applied in the real world.

The results

Net profit in the first half of the second year was an impressive $48 million on a turnover of $600 million. But what interested Dick Davis was the first full set of 'horizontal accounts', and these were now ready. A board meeting had been called to discuss the results, but only the 'traditional' set of accounts had been circulated prior to the meeting. These did of course show the huge improvement in net profit.

VCL Limited Profit & Loss Account 6 Months	$m Total	Reseller	Distributor	Direct
Sales of Products	500.0	240.0	140.0	120.0
Maintenance	24.0	0	0	24.0
Other Services	76.0	24.0	12.0	40.0
Total Sales	600.0	264.0	152.0	184.0
Less: Cost of Sales	349.6	184.8	91.2	73.6
Gross Profit	250.4	79.2	60.8	110.4
Distribution Expenses	120.0	53.2	30.0	36.8
Administration Expenses	60.0	29.6	12.0	18.4
Operating Profit	70.4	(3.6)	18.8	55.2
Less: Interest	22.0	9.7	5.6	6.8
Profit before Tax	48.4	(13.3)	13.2	48.5

Bill Burgess had not yet seen the horizontal accounts but was delighted with the half-year's results. He opened the meeting.

CHAIRMAN: Well, suddenly everyone wants to talk to us – what a turnaround! I've only one negative comment on the figures and I'm afraid it's the usual one – what the hell are we going to do with the reseller channel? Our accounts show that without it we would be making a far greater profit. Tom, what's your view on this?

FINANCE DIRECTOR: Bill, as you rightly suggest, these accounts point clearly to the closure of the reseller channel. But we've just produced the first results from our new system and they show a radically different picture. I'm sorry that you haven't had them earlier, but we were working on them late into the evening. We wanted to make sure we'd not made any stupid errors. *(hands out copies of the horizontal accounts)*

VCL Limited $m Horizontal Profit Statement 6 Months	Total	Reseller	Distributor	Direct
Total Sales	**600.0**	**264.0**	**152.0**	**184.0**
Direct Costs	349.6	184.8	91.2	73.6
Overheads	46.4	11.4	9.0	26.0
Profit after Specific Costs	**204.0**	**67.8**	**51.8**	**84.4**
Process Overheads	50.4	14.0	8.0	28.4
Support Costs	36.0	11.6	4.4	20.0
Capital Costs	22.0	8.0	4.0	10.0
Quality Costs	47.2	12.0	11.2	24.0
Horizontal Profit	**48.4**	**22.2**	**24.2**	**2.0**
Total Non-Value-Adding Costs	126.0	36.8	23.4	65.8
Value-Adding Work Index	77.2%	84.8%	81.7%	63.8%

CHAIRMAN: Dick, what do you make of these figures?

CEO: Bill, I can see you're a bit surprised. Why don't I go through the new report?

CHAIRMAN: Good idea.

CEO: In all our previous management reports we've allocated channel overheads by volume, and, as you can see from the first report, because the reseller channel has almost twice the sales and volume of the other two channels, it received a much higher proportion of overheads. This resulted in the regular attributable losses to the reseller channel that you've seen up to now. In the horizontal accounts – up to gross profit level – the results are similar to our previous estimates.

Look at the chart which compares the traditional profits with the revised horizontal profits. You can see, for example, that the loss of $13.3m in the reseller channel has now turned into a profit of $22m, while the high profit of the direct channel has almost disappeared.

CHAIRMAN: What's happened to cause this change?

CEO: As you know, the gross profits we make on our direct sales are high because we don't have to give extra discounts. However, under the horizontal accounts it's crystal clear that the majority of our overhead costs are spent looking after the very demanding needs of our direct customers. For example, they demand special deliveries and a great deal of preconfiguring, that is, they want us to put the whole system together for them before we ship it. This can be very time consuming, particularly when it involves additional memory and the preloading of software. Nor are we able to recover all these extra costs because our customers tell us that they can get similar terms from the competition. On the other hand, dealers and distributors merely send us an order which goes straight to the warehouse for picking, and out it goes! Look at the report on the costs of quality.

CEO: Tom, can you explain this report to us?

FINANCE DIRECTOR: The real clue to the problems in the direct channel is the high level of quality-related costs which are summarised on this report. These costs represent all the chasing, problem solving and extra work everyone has to do, because we're not getting things right first time. You can see that many of the production problems are caused by direct customers who demand changes to products all through the production process. But we are beginning to make

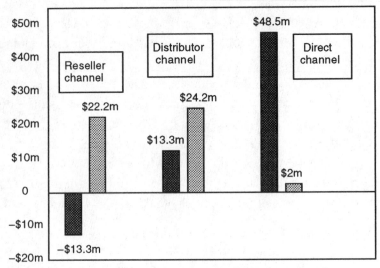

Traditional profits compared with horizontal profits

VCL Limited Non-value-adding Costs Cost Summary (over $1m)	$m Total	Reseller	Distributor	Direct
Maintain bill of materials	4.0	1.3	0.9	1.8
Change routing	2.0	0.1	0.6	1.3
Engineering change orders	7.2	1.3	1.9	4.0
Defective components	4.0	0.5	1.1	2.4
Incorrect inbound deliveries	4.8	0.9	1.2	2.7
Production bottlenecks	3.6	0.4	1.0	2.2
Sales order corrections	3.6	0.6	1.0	2.0
Incorrect outbound deliveries	4.0	0.3	1.2	2.5
Technical support (waste)	4.0	1.1	0.9	2.0
Service parts not available	5.0	2.2	0.8	2.0
Others (under $1m)	5.0	3.3	0.6	1.1
Costs of Poor Quality	47.2	12.0	11.2	24.0

progress with these costs. A number of improvement targets have already been established.

CEO: Bill, perhaps I should put these accounts into some sort of context. First, although they are not yet perfect by any means, I believe they show the real performance of the business. For the first time we can see the costs of quality, and we can see the full impact of non-value-adding costs. The true extent of this really shows up if you look at the 'value-adding work index' at the bottom of the report. This gives us a rough and ready measure, by account, by process, and by the company as a whole, of the proportion of our costs which are of value to customers. You can see that the overall performance index for the company is 77 per cent. Looked at a different way, it shows that 23 per cent of our total costs, or $126 million, add no value for our customers. Of this total, roughly 60 per cent is accounted for by 'unproductive time' – or work which is simply not relevant – and 40 per cent is accounted for by poor quality. It also enables us to highlight more detailed areas where the value of work is quite low, and investigate further how it can be improved. In fact, we have a number of such investigations in progress at the present time. Incidentally, the profit statement only shows the poor quality aspect of non-value-adding work. At this stage we have taken the view that the cost of irrelevant work is more subjective and therefore should only be shown as a note to the accounts.

CHAIRMAN: Dick, I can see you're excited by this report – and quite understandably. But what other factors would you pick out in the overall improvement in these figures?

CEO: One that springs to mind immediately is the way our salespeople now deal with customers. For example, we've radically changed the sales incentive scheme to reward customer net profitability, which is quite a departure from the previous policy of rewarding gross revenue. In fact, we've noticed that our sales force have taken up much of our time with requests for information on customer profitability, but they tell us that this information has strengthened their hand in all negotiations with customers. Some unprofitable customers have gone elsewhere, but our salespeople now take the view that if these customers are using the time of our competitors — instead of wasting ours – then the way is clear for us to sell to customers who produce the real profits. It's interesting to observe how our salespeople are now much more aware of the 'business case' when negotiating with customers.

CHAIRMAN: Good. Anything else?

CEO: With our new horizontal information systems now firmly in place, we can measure the real work that we do. For instance, our research and design people know that they have to create new products within agreed cost and time parameters and not just produce clever, award-winning products. But they also know that value-adding time is more important than raw cost. In fact the whole mentality of the firm is now tuned in to the need to ensure that all costs are only committed if they benefit customers. The only proviso is that they take the company towards its strategic targets.

CHAIRMAN: One other change is noticeable – our employees now take delight in talking to customers. In the bad old days, many of us would avoid customer contact if possible, because we knew it would be 'earache' all the way – one problem after another. We now know that our customers are well satisfied with our products and services. In my view one of the most important changes is the way we now measure customer retention and defection levels – the first sign of a customer not buying from us is picked up and investigated. We solve any problem on the spot (our customer service people have wide discretion) and we are now winning most of these customers back. But Dick, I have to ask you to explain how costs have fallen so dramatically. Our efforts over recent years have been abject failures. How have you done it, and what other changes are important?

CEO: You don't need to be Pythagoras to work out that with lower turnover, a large increase in profits, and a static workforce, something serious has changed – and it has to be a significant reduction in costs. But the key is that those costs that have gone are those that previously added no value for our customers. They were the costs of reworks, changes, revisits, reprocessing, and a million and one other aspects of work that had to be done more than once. Now most of our work – done by the roughly the same number of people, although the mix of people and work has changed – is only done once, and the reduction in costs is dramatic.

But even in this area we are only part way there. Our new horizontal information system now tracks measures of quality and work performance, and these reports tell our team leaders pretty quickly if any work needs improvement. The system can also trace the source of any faulty work, which enables the offending team leader to take corrective action. We've set ambitious targets to further improve the performance of our work over the next few years. The productivity dividends should continue to be spectacular for quite a while yet.

The other major area of improvement has been in the use of our intellectual assets. We've recently adapted our horizontal information systems to highlight organisational learning. Any time now spent by our 'knowledge people' on improving standards, processes, systems and overall competence, is rewarded by applying a 150 per cent rating to that piece of work. This gives them the recognition they deserve and enables us to measure how much time and cost is spent throughout the firm on these activities. Anyone with a 150 per cent rating now regards themselves as part of the premier league of workers within the company.

Finally, and crucially, the cultural change has been remarkable. From the ingrained parochial attitudes that pervaded the organisation two years ago, I now find a confident team-based approach to all important issues. Not only has it been like learning a new language, but learning to think in a new language. The questions asked by our managers are now far more relevant to the competitive battles we constantly have to fight.

Postscript

The following year Dick Davis called back to see the team at VCL. Tom Moore was now chief executive. Profit figures for the third year of the transformation programme were about to be released and they were amazing. New products were coming on stream at a fast and furious pace, but profit was dramatically boosted by the driving down of non-value-adding work. The value-adding-work index for the year was now up to 88 per cent, saving $60 million of costs over the previous year.

Dick was left with one final thought. If the underlying issues in any organisation are properly tackled and the information systems point in the right direction (i.e. horizontally towards the customer), the performance of the business doesn't depend on one or two special people. Of course leadership is important, but good, solid managers can all make sensible decisions if they have the right information to hand.

9

MANAGING THE TRANSFORMATION PROGRAMME

Most corporations are like giant jellies. You can force them briefly into a new shape. But unless you can fundamentally reform the culture that holds them together – the personal skills of middle management, for example – they swiftly wobble back into their old form.

Richard Heygate

THE TRANSFORMATION MESSAGE IS CLEAR. ORGANISATIONS MUST REDUCE the work*load* not the work*force*; improve the speed and quality of their processes; create a management structure that looks to the customer; promote value-adding work and the spread of knowledge; and use well-designed information systems to guide them. While the imperatives may be clear, putting them into practice is less easy. This final chapter considers the issues at stake.

The transformation programme is primarily about one objective: creating long-term success. It is not simply doing better what is done today, but anticipating competitive conditions in future years and gearing the organisation accordingly. Hamel and Pralahad agree:

Catching up is not enough. In a survey taken at the end of the 1980s, nearly 80% of US managers polled believed that quality would be a fundamental source of competitive advantage in the year 2000, but barely half of Japanese managers agreed. Their primary goal was to create new products and businesses. Does this mean that Japanese managers will turn their backs on quality? Of course not. It merely indicates that by the year 2000, quality will be the price of market entry, not a competitive differentiator.

Many executive teams are unable to translate their beliefs and ideas into a practical programme. To be successful, the organisation must share a common purpose and converse in a common language. McKinsey & Co looked in detail at over 30 major transformation programmes. They placed the issue of language and purpose in context:

> The right conversation is essential. Which in turn means having in place a shared *framework* for structuring activities and responsibilities, a *road map* for laying out their proper sequence, and a background set of *guiding principles* about the 'natural laws' that govern organisational transformations. All three of them – framework, road map, and guiding principles – are necessary for a successful conversation, because all three have a critical role to play in giving CEOs the practical means to shepherd through a balanced, integrated change programme.

But changing ingrained attitudes, implementing new information systems, penetrating powerful management cliques, and convincing knowledge workers to share their assets constitute a formidable pro-gramme. For example, a statement such as 'we are making changes to improve internal processes and customer value' sounds quite different from 'we have to make cuts to survive and this is how we're doing it'. Most transformation programmes start on the wrong foot. And because they often follow in the wake of failed restructuring efforts that have left indelible scars on the workforce, they are seen as just another attempt at cost reduction.

FOCUS ON PEOPLE AND PROCESSES

While organisations frequently boast of their total commitment to quality, service and improving the skills of their people, the reality suggests otherwise. Chapter 1 reminded us that McGregor's Theory X philosophy remains the prevailing influence over managerial actions, and that its ramifications are felt in the traditional accounting systems which are the measurement tools of the command and control organisation. But as Drucker has noted, the new organisation must be designed around an open information system rather than a control philosophy:

> The command and control organisation that first emerged in the 1870s might be compared to an organism held together by its shell. The corporation that is now emerging is being designed around a skeleton: *information*, both the corporation's new integrating systems and its articulation.

One of Drucker's more recently argued themes is that knowledge and service workers are in the vanguard of the new productivity revolution and that organisations need both to understand their problems and protect their interests. But, as already argued, accounting and reward systems do not usually support the interests of knowledge and service workers. More often than not, they undermine them. The time which knowledge workers actually spend on creative work is dismally low, and service workers are, more often than not, seen as costs rather than as the key providers of customer satisfaction. The transformation programme needs to address this issue by removing unnecessary work from their schedules and placing more emphasis on speed of development rather than on meeting cost targets. At chemical firm Process Plus, for example, by reducing the time that scientists spent at unnecessary meetings, the value-adding content of their work tripled from 5 to 15 per cent.

But executives are on the horns of a dilemma. With the value of their firms increasingly based around the intelligence and ideas of their people rather than capabilities of their more traditional and tangible assets, investors are backing brains rather than balance sheets. But these 'brains' are now marketable commodities. Managers are now asking how they can be retained and how their creativity can be maximised. The answers do not fit easily with a control philosophy.

Charles Handy has suggested that to nurture creativity and guarantee excellent service, organisations must look to a different form of contract with their workers – more akin to a club whose members work towards agreed goals but whose collective rights cannot easily be overridden. Such notions, however, are likely to be anathema to executives and shareholders more used to buying and selling companies than investing for long-term success. In a membership constitution the organisation (like the club) cannot be sold against the wishes of its members, nor can major strategic initiatives and capital programmes be undertaken without their support.

However, this type of structure offers many potential benefits. Indeed, the concept of membership works both ways. For example, members are more likely to 'own' their targets, take responsibility for their actions, and participate in improvement programmes if they have a stake in the business. Long-term investors can be seen as part of the extended family of the club-based organisation – a relationship not unfamiliar to Japanese and German investors and family companies elsewhere. As Handy suggests:

> The concept of membership, when made real, would replace the sense of belonging to a *place* with the sense of belonging to a *community*, even if that community were a largely virtual one. A sense of belonging is something that humans need if they are to commit themselves to more than simple selfishness. Families and family businesses know something about the sense of belonging and the motivating force of collective pride in the family tradition as well as the responsibilities that go with belonging. Families, at their best, are communities based on trust. If the family could be extended to include key contributors, the sense of belonging would be properly inclusive.

Handy's ideas, however, seem more than a little futuristic for most organisations. Nevertheless, the question of the right business structure has to be faced. Can the transformation architect make minor changes to the existing structure and maintain a credible transformation programme? Or does the high-rise monolith need to be replaced with a single-storey structure which faces horizontally towards the customer? Judging by the actions of many leading-edge companies, moves in the latter direction hold out more promise of success.

The model which is being increasingly advocated is built around a small number of key business processes which deliver high quality products and services to the customer. And the building blocks of this structure are teams. Teams must be vested with the power and responsibility to satisfy customer needs and to set their own performance measures to meet them. Executives and specialist functions must exist to support these team-based efforts. And the remote and often authoritative head office must cease to be the centre of organisational gravity. This point was made in a recent article on the successful changes at BP Oil:

> The 'new style' head office, and the collective behaviours that it promotes, will change the culture of the whole company. With reduced layers of hierarchy and smaller permanent staff departments, it is inevitable that managers will move to project-based jobs. Career paths must be found in the operating units, not at the centre and horizontal moves become career-enhancing, not limiting. Functional specialists will have few opportunities to manage departments but must persuade and influence their internal customers. Above all, managers must be more open and trusting and find new motivation in the challenges of continuous improvement and teamworking.

Good communication and information sharing are crucial to the successful implementation of a team-based structure. At Lincoln Electric, for example, information is shared with all employees regarding the financial and market position of the organisation. Executives must set strategy and teams must carry it out. Objectives should be clearly set and well communicated. As one study on transformation programmes put it:

Organisations can perform well with less than perfect strategies, but not with unclear objectives. Especially during periods of change, it is easy to let attention drift away from tangible performance goals toward a more general concern for effecting the necessary shifts in organisational culture. But this puts things the wrong way round. The best way to change culture is to work on improving performance at the same time.

Rewards must also be changed to support team-based efforts. The individual incentive culture must be consigned to the scrapheap. As Deming has argued:

> The merit rating nourishes short-term performance, annihilates long-term planning, builds fear, demolishes teamwork, and nourishes rivalry and politics.

SUCCEEDING IN TRANSFORMATION

Even with the benefit of team-based structures, horizontal information systems and the right philosophy and language, much still needs to be done to transform the bottom line successfully. The transformation programme itself has to be properly managed. Successful changes proceed step by step. Indeed, the transformation journey itself is essentially a learning process. The general manager at one of the Volvo car plants had this experience:

> We didn't know this was where we were going when we started. We just sat down and began to talk, developed some new ideas and tried them out. When we saw what was successful we would extend it. It took much patience and a willingness to move one step at a time and see where it led. This kind of process is demanding on management and workers alike. Many times we asked ourselves, 'Shall we go on?'

Managing change requires special skills which are rarely found. Indeed, major changes are often planned in secret, and once the final plan has been agreed a coordinated announcement is made to the assembled masses. In the meantime, rumour and gossip fill the vacuum, with expectations of the worst to come. When the news breaks, employees feel alienated and resistance is more likely than compliance. This approach almost guarantees failure. Two-way communication is crucial to success. The UK Automobile Association, one of the largest motorist support organisations in the world, transformed its business in the early 1990s. One of the keys to success was the ability of workers to communicate upwards. By introducing in-house magazines, phone-ins (with the guarantee of an answer) and discussion groups, workers were given a voice. According to group managing director Bob Chase:

> All these moves have helped to empower staff and to boost their confidence, and they played a critical part in the success of the AA during the recession. The results of the changes speak for themselves. We reduced duplication and administration, 90% of our problems are now solved by innovative local teams. And there has been a significant improvement in the quality of member service.

Few companies have succeeded in the transformation effort without setting up a special group to oversee the process. UK bank TSB plc, with 33,500 staff and 7 million customers, conducted their reorganisation in this way. The new management team led by Peter Ellwood created a new vision and evolved a strategy for carrying it out. They transformed the company by a series of actions, one of which was the creation of a project team to manage the process. According to Ellwood:

> I believe that the only way effectively to bring about large scale radical change is to divorce the action of change from the day to day process of management. Responsibility for delivering the change should be given to dedicated, focused project teams using rigorous project management methodology.

But long-term success will not come from the efforts of project management teams alone (important though they are). It will come from setting clear objectives, developing a common language, and using an open information system based on trust. It is here that horizontal information systems have a crucial role to play. But they must be seen as a support structure for team building and reward setting, not as a new accounting tool of control.

The issue of employee 'buy-in' is crucial, particularly when new methods of accounting, which are inevitably viewed with suspicion, are to be introduced. Horizontal systems will enjoy a smoother ride if they are presented as better methods of tracking and reporting on customer-based performance than simply as a new and better accounting system. Their success will depend on worker understanding and commitment, and on a clear comprehension of which work adds value. Although this looks like a tall order, there are some success stories. At New United Motor Manufacturing (NUMMI) – the highly successful joint venture between GM and Toyota – employees are taught how to break down jobs into their component parts, analyse them and search for efficiencies.

The transformation in performance at NUMMI, compared with that of the GM business in the same location which preceded it, is truly startling. By reemploying most of the previous workers the NUMMI management created a new language, a new philosophy and a new agenda. On every comparative measure available, including comparisons against the best Japanese car plants, NUMMI's performance was exemplary. Above all, employees had a clear understanding of the measurement approach:

> GM had no real production system...at least nothing that people on the shop floor ever saw... At NUMMI, we've got a comprehensive system that ties together in a defined and disciplined way standardised work, just-in-time inventory, preventive maintenance, quality control – a system that everyone on that shop floor understands and respects.

One recent article put the change management process as follows:

> Want a tough job? Try leading an organisation through major change – a merger say, or reengineering, or a devolution from a hierarchy to teams. Almost without exception, executives claim it's the hardest work they've ever done.

But it is also important to understand that changes is not just something that an organisation has to deal with – reluctantly – every now and then. *Change is now part of the very fabric of business life* and must be supported by accounting systems.

Three paradoxes face the leaders of the transformation process:

❑ Everyone must have a voice, but cynics must be silenced. The most ardent foes of change are those with the most to lose. According to one executive, these are the people who 'want to drag you back to the comfort zone'. The answer is to scatter the cynics among executive task forces.

❑ Without taking their eyes off the horizon, leaders must watch where they step. Such a paradox bedevilled Lou Gerstner shortly after he joined IBM, when he said 'the last thing IBM needs right now is a vision'. Most transformation leaders stress the importance of vision and mission statements but, as already argued, an excessive focus on vision can mean that leaders fail to see that they are being driven off course by other forces (e.g. by budgeting and reward systems).

❑ Change is scary, but people volunteer for dangerous tasks only when they feel safe. For a long-term transformation programme to succeed, people need to cope with many changes – in the way their work is carried out, how they are measured, and how they are rewarded. But at the same time, for this new programme to work and to gain commitment from the workforce, people must feel safe and secure in their new roles. Al Dunlop, CEO of Scott Paper, asked the obvious question: 'Who can work in an environment where you say you're going to restructure over the next three years?' Safety can be created in a team-based structure by teams themselves taking ownership and responsibility for their performance. Then it is down to them.

HORIZONTAL SYSTEMS PROVIDE THE GLUE

Any programme for transforming the bottom line cannot be represented by one unique masterplan. It must fit in with other improvement programmes such as total quality, reengineering and organisational learning. Indeed, it is likely that parts of the transformation programme will require these approaches. For example, the only way to improve some processes is to reengineer them. Horizontal systems offer managers a new opportunity to bring out the best from these project-based approaches and integrate their results within one measurement system.

Connecting with other improvement programmes

Many solutions to deep-rooted business problems have been proposed (and implemented) over recent years, but have often been thwarted by the hidden barriers of accounting and reward systems. Moreover, they are all too often seen as 'projects' which, by definition, are ephemeral. These programmes are often uncoordinated and unconnected, especially when attempts are made to measure bottom-line results. As one article suggested:

> The difficulty of connecting [improvement] activities to the bottom line
> is complicated by the fact that most companies choose to launch a vast
> array of activities simultaneously across the entire organisation. This is
> like researching a cure for a disease by giving a group of patients ten
> different new drugs at the same time.

To deliver on the promises, improvement programmes need a common measurement framework. Horizontal systems provide such a framework (see Figure 9.1). They connect with these programmes in various ways.

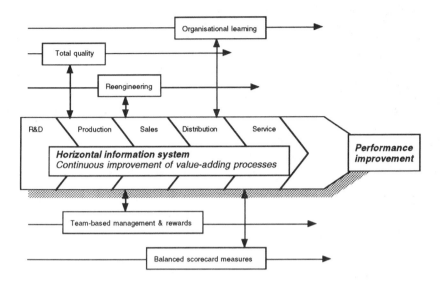

Figure 9.1   Connecting improvement programmes to a horizontal information system

❑ *Total quality management (TQM)*. It was noted earlier that account-ing systems often collide with TQM programmes primarily because they encourage the recovery of overheads by maximising volume, whereas the TQM approach favours small batches, minimal work in progress and production to demand. Nor do traditional information systems highlight or reward improvements in cycle times, lower defects or faster deliveries. By connecting TQM programmes with a horizontal system, time and cost saved can be systematically measured and improvements monitored.

❑ *Reengineering*. Reengineering programmes are often unsuccessful, and accountants have seldom been able to measure their results. But horizontal systems are a natural partner to reengineering pro-grammes. They both focus on process improvement – reengineering on the means and horizontal systems on the means and the measures – and both require a focus on managing activities.

❑ *Activity-based management*. Most ABM programmes struggle to col-lect data and often fail because they are piecemeal and project driven.

Horizontal systems, with their emphasis on the systematic collection of data, can bring existing ABM systems to life.

❏ *Balanced scorecard measures*. Existing measurement systems, of which the balanced scorecard is perhaps the most advanced example, focus on results rather than on how they were achieved. Horizontal systems can help to analyse the performance of business processes more effectively by continuously reporting on value-adding work and pinpointing where and why problems occur.

❏ *Team-based structures*. Horizontal structures need horizontal systems. The two go hand in glove. Many team-based structures have failed because managers have not changed the orientation of their accounting systems.

❏ *Organisational learning*. Horizontal systems can support the spread of knowledge by measuring and promoting time spent by workers in pursuit of this objective.

The objective is to transform the bottom line

Once executives become intimately involved with major change programmes they can easily lose sight of their main objective – to improve long-term profitability. This lack of focus was evident in one leading US corporation where researchers found that a group of quality facilitators could not articulate their unit's critical business goals. When asked how they could possibly assess whether or not they were successful, they replied that success consisted of getting 100 per cent of each unit's managers and employees to attend the prescribed quality training – a centrepiece of the corporation's total quality programme.

What results should be expected from a transformation programme with a horizontal system at its core? The following list suggests possible benefits for those willing to go down the horizontal road:

❏ *Processes will be improved and costs reduced*. Once non-value-adding costs (particularly of poor quality) are made visible to managers, corrective action can be taken and the root causes eradicated. Their removal will increase process speed and cut process costs.

❑ *Productivity will be improved.* A horizontal information system, and the measures which can be derived from it (in particular the value-adding work index) addresses the key issues of productivity and value creation. By measuring and rewarding improvements in the *value of work to customers*, managers will focus their energies on the productivity of individuals, teams, processes and business units. Productivity improvements of ten times have been suggested as the potential magnitude of the change from a traditional to a team-based structure.

❑ *Organisational learning can be promoted.* Horizontal information systems have the capability to plan, track and reward individual pieces of work. Indeed, premiums can be placed on certain activities if they involve the dissemination of knowledge throughout the organisation.

❑ *Managers will make better decisions.* Horizontal systems give managers the opportunity to derive net profitability by product, customer, channel and business unit. Knowing which costs to cut, which products and services to expand and contract, and which sales channels to choose will be easier if managers can distinguish between value-adding and non-value-adding costs. A clearer understanding of product and customer profitability can only help managers understand the source of their organisation's profits.

❑ *More appropriate reward and recognition systems can be implemented.* A number of companies are now realising that the only effort really worth rewarding is that which adds value for customers. However, such possible reward systems cannot be invoked without the information to support them. Once horizontal information systems are in place, there is scope for implementing reward and incentive systems that drive the company towards its strategic targets. For example, IBM and other computer companies have begun to reward salespeople on measures of customer profitability and customer satisfaction.

❑ *Forward planning will be improved.* By budgeting for work instead of costs, managers are forced to seek answers to a new (and more relevant) set of questions. And value-adding behaviour will be encouraged where it counts – before costs are committed.

This list is not intended to suggest that horizontal systems can, on their own, bring success, any more than can reengineering or quality initiatives. But they might just be the missing piece in the jigsaw – the piece that brings the whole transformation picture into focus. The design of such systems depends on the imaginative use of information technology.

INFORMATION TECHNOLOGY HOLDS THE KEY

Unless executives and process teams receive the performance reports they require, when they require them, the programme will be handicapped. But in a constantly changing world, the definition of these requirements is a difficult task and the response of IT managers, whose technology-dominated world is changing equally quickly, has often been vague. Paralysis and frustration with the software development process have often been the result. The problem with the choice of IT solution lies in the number of available paths. Whether to adapt existing systems, to buy in software packages, to outsource development, or to develop customised solutions in-house (and what approach to take in such development) are all possible options, and each has major implications for cost, timescale and the satisfaction of user needs. While these are difficult choices, and the circumstances of each firm will undoubtedly be different, a number of general (but important) criteria must be satisfied if the transformation programme is to be successful.

The system design must be derived from and support strategic objectives

Although many organisations have spent vast sums of money on IT over recent years, most systems have failed to support the strategic goals of the business. Indeed, after the spending boom of the 1980s many executives were left wondering where were the fruits of their massive investments. In a recent article, Davenport argued:

Information technology has a polarising effect on managers; it either bedazzles or frightens. Those who are afraid of it shun it, while bedazzled. IT departments frequently become prisoners of their own fascination, constructing elaborate technology architectures and enterprise-wide information models to guide systems development.

Until recently, enterprise-wide systems driven from the centre of the organisation were thought to be the way forward. But with constantly changing business processes it was recognised as unlikely that these large centrally driven systems could be implemented before they were overtaken by events. In other words, designing solutions to deal with cycle times and quality issues might well address important strategic objectives, but will be useless if they take five years to develop.

In fact, in many cases driving IT development from the centre of the organisation has proved to be a disaster. Rank Xerox, for example, abandoned its attempts in the 1980s to generate computer models for enterprise-wide systems – in the course of the project technicians lost their way, and the project's original purpose was buried beneath the technical challenge. Now the company designs specific and more localised systems. Failure to understand the needs of users, and the slow speed of development, seem to be recurrent criticisms of IT departments. Much of this problem stems from the limited development time available. In several companies served by McKinsey, for example, only 7–10 per cent of IT time is available for new developments – the remaining 90 per cent or so is required simply to maintain old applications.

Systems should support the team-based structure

Traditional large IT systems have been highly centralised and detached from customer needs. Indeed, it is now increasingly recognised that successful IT systems will be developed within such operational units as process teams. Only by reducing the distance between specialists and users will IT begin to be an obedient slave rather than an erratic and inflexible master. Teams – with their integral IT capability – have the answer. Only teams can understand the systems they require to meet their objectives and make decisions on the consequent scope, timescale, investment and measurements.

Thus just as executives set strategy and teams implement, so the specialist IT function will set IT strategy, define common standards (databases, languages, communication protocols, etc.), and support team-based developments. Specialist functions, with their role as guardians of organisational standards and their monitoring of the external competitive environment, have an important part to play in IT strategy by providing this support.

Systems must be able to analyse and record value-adding and non-value-adding costs

At the core of the horizontal data system lie activities, and it is the ability to analyse activity costs as 'value-adding' and 'non-value-adding' that is critical to the success of a horizontal information system. Such analysis depends on the ability (and willingness) of people to record their 'negative', or non-value-adding, time. To capture this information at the point of its occurrence is vital, otherwise such knowledge will be prone to distortion and lapses of memory. The use of a range of data-capture devices is important, from simple notepads to sophisticated radio-controlled (hand-held) devices.

It is doubtful that, initially, managers or designers will know all the right questions to be asked of a horizontal information system. So the design must be flexible and able both to integrate new ideas and cope with significant changes. Activity analysis is one example where such flexibility is essential. For example, the definition and choice of an activity are likely to change as working methods evolve. Therefore the system design must cope with both the possible combination of two or more activities into a larger one (and carry their data with them), and the splitting of one activity into smaller bundles (again transferring activity data accordingly). The size or scale of an activity are meaningless to a computer system.

Once costs have been classified as value-adding and non-value-adding, they must be traced through the activity ledger to reporting categories. Such categories are likely to be multi-dimensional. For example, information on products and customers needs to be held by: product, product group, sales area, distribution channel, customer group, market segment and business unit. Similarly, work might be analysed by: person, team, activity, division, market, product, customer and business unit. Multi-dimensional databases enable such information to be analysed, stored and held available for instant enquiry.

Systems must enable users to see the 'whole information picture'

Historically, computer systems have evolved around business functions such as manufacturing, distribution, finance, maintenance and service. Thus, most managers still cannot deal with a query by informing the customer immediately what is currently being produced for the customer, whether it has already been shipped, or whether payment has been received. Banks have a similar problem. They typically have different systems for current accounts, loans and mortgages, and investments. So in direct contact with a customer, a manager cannot quickly see the complete picture of the customer's position with the bank. One of the principal aims of horizontal information systems will be to provide users with a more complete picture of the subject under examination, whether it be a customer, a product, the performance of any part of the business, or any combination of these. To achieve this, managers must be able to view a customer account by financial status (including sales, costs and net profitability); operational status (e.g. quality, speed, efficiency, satisfaction); and background (e.g. history, trends and predictions).

Systems should encourage information sharing and promote organisational learning

In a transformed organisation, information will be shared. But such sharing will not come naturally. Employees are frequently uncomfortable with such arrangements and prefer to keep sensitive information (and knowledge) to themselves, particularly if they perceive that their power and influence within the organisation rest on the processing of this knowledge.

Managers must understand that people are at the centre of information systems, and systems must be designed to fit their needs. They must understand why information is needed and how it will benefit them. The closer employees are to the design and development of systems and the setting of performance targets, the more likely they are to participate enthusiastically in IT initiatives.

Managers also need to share knowledge and experience within their own organisation. Hughes Aircraft is one firm that is investing in its own 'knowledge highway', by trying to encourage knowledge workers to share their experiences through groupware technology. According to Adrian Ward, leader of business reengineering, 'people think in terms of stories, not facts'.

External information sources are now vast and wide-ranging, but this very abundance has created its own problems. For example, how is the source of the desired information to be located? A number of companies have recently created information 'maps' showing how to locate sources (IBM, for example, has prepared its own information guides and catalogues). Knowledge sharing is now a major issue. Coopers & Lybrand first addressed this issue in 1989 by installing 'groupware' facilities which comprise electronic mail, document management and bulletin boards, but it is only recently that the system has really caught on and now 28,000 users are connected.

Systems must be developed with minimum cost and disruption

Managers must develop systems at the lowest levels of cost and disruption compatible with attaining satisfactory levels of achievement. If possible, they should try to expand and extend existing systems rather than create entirely new ones. In their pursuit of the perfect solution (irrespective of cost and time constraints), IT developers can easily become detached both from the real world of users, and the costs of development. According to McKinsey this can result in IT departments:

spending a great deal of time solving technical problems that bring only marginal benefit. A good rule of thumb is that 80% or so of the value of any system can be captured relatively quickly and easily – and that the remaining 20% can often be so hard to capture as to be not worth pursuing.

This issue goes to the heart of the IT debate – how much value to the business can IT deliver, and can this extra value be justified in time and cost? In a horizontal system this question relates not only to investment in the system infrastructure, but also to the use of 'personal technology'. In particular, firms must invest in an appropriate range of data capture tools and devices. The reliability and usefulness of data (and thus its ultimate credibility) depend on the accuracy and timeliness of source data.

Managers shouldn't expect too much too quickly. Tracing costs to products and customers will not always be easy. But, to use an old cliché, it is better to be approximately right than precisely wrong. For example, products and customers can be 'banded' together into groups according to the approximate level of resources they use. Just as general ledger analysis evolved over time (from the simple 'one-level view' of years ago to the multi-layered, detailed analysis of today), so activity analysis will improve as managers learn to use the new horizontal information system.

EVOLUTION, NOT REVOLUTION

It is 500 years since Luca Pacioli wrote his masterpiece, *Summa de Arithmetica, Geometrica, Proportioni et Proportionilitia*, in which he expounded his thesis on double entry book-keeping. He wrote:

> It is necessary that all a businessman's affairs be arranged in a systematic way so that he may get at their particulars at a glance... without systematic recording, their minds would always be so tired and troubled that it would be impossible for them to conduct business.

Pacioli's dictum seems as appropriate today as it did in the late fifteenth century. There must be a lot of tired and troubled minds in today's business community as managers try to come to terms with the problems caused by a fast-changing world. But many have tried and achieved a remarkable degree of success.

This success suggests (quite rightly) that the transformation agenda is not necessarily one whole, indivisible package. As many companies have testified, huge performance improvements can be gained by adopting just one or two of the proposals. GE and Hewlett-Packard, for example, have made great strides in understanding the causes of costs and have embraced horizontal structures, begun to eliminate non-value-adding work and improved employee productivity. GE is now the number one company in the western world in terms of market capitalisation, and HP's recent profits growth has been both impressive and consistent in an intensely competitive market. Companies such as Motorola and Xerox have realised substantial benefits from adopting horizontal team-based structures, involving the removal of multiple layers of management and resulting in both a reduction in costs and much improved service levels.

Many companies have adopted more relevant performance measures and begun to understand and appreciate how customers see their business. Apple, Rockwater and a number of leading British banks have successfully embraced the balanced scorecard, and begun to relate performance to strategy. Royal Bank of Canada, Arthur Andersen and IBM now use non-financial measures to reward management performance. Many firms now implement price-led costing techniques. Retailers such as Wal-Mart in America and Sainsbury's in the UK have become experts in this field, and Marks & Spencer, Britain's best known retailer, has been using these methods successfully for years.

Japanese manufacturers have demonstrated the power of target costing and the benefits of building partnerships with suppliers and customers throughout the entire value chain. Toyota, Nissan, NEC and others have led the way in developing continuous improvement techniques which involve chipping away at non-value-adding work.

Although few companies appear to understand how to measure customer profitability, most understand the need for top-quality service.

British Airways and Southwest Airlines have developed a reputation for service and their profits are outstanding. Ford Motor, MBNA and Ritz-Carlton have all recognised the extent to which extra profits are to be gained from the retention of customers. And Federal Express, Lincoln Electric and NUMMI have built hugely successful businesses by placing the commitment and satisfaction of employees at their heart.

There are many more examples, too numerous to list, but each one deals with only part of the transformation agenda. There are, however, others who have missed the boat. The continuous cost cutters who have reduced jobs and closed companies, offices and factories in every town and city throughout Europe and America have still not come to terms with their underlying problems. They need to be convinced that there is a better and more coherent way for changes to be made. We believe that our programme offers this.

However, most organisations remain prisoners of their accounting systems and management structures. The introduction of a horizontal information system offers them new hope. Horizontal systems provide managers with a new framework for measuring the real performance of the business. Strategy, satisfaction, quality, work, innovation and time rarely appear in the accountant's lexicon. But they must now be added. New systems must be designed to bring these words to life. By highlighting value creation, eliminating unnecessary work, and using technology to improve the speed and quality of processes and information systems, firms can release a powerful surge of energy to fuel the momentum of growth and profitability for years to come. Increasing the productivity of work, providing more value for the customer, measuring the results of strategic decisions and reducing the right costs, must be major parts of the virtuous circle every organisation is searching for – but without suitable measurement systems this isn't likely to happen.

The philosophy of control must be challenged and replaced. Managers need to become more positive in their pursuit of systems which measure strategic targets. They must believe such systems are possible. They can no longer hide behind the mystique of large, inflexible computer systems, nor within the safe haven of well tried and tested methods of cost accounting. The changes proposed in this book won't be

REFERENCES

Chapter 1

Page 1: *Accounts can measure* – Robert Heller, *The Leadership Imperative*, Truman Talley Books/Dutton, New York, 1995.

Page 1: *a recent CA-I report* – *A Journey to Advanced Management System: A Report on the Research and Findings of the CAM-I Advanced Budgeting Group*, CAM-I Inc, September 1994.

Page 3: *In their 1987 book* – H Thomas Johnson and Robert S Kaplan, 1987, *Relevance Lost: The Rise and Fall of Management Accounting*, Harvard Business School Press.

Page 4: *If something was simple* – Michael Hammer and James Champy, 1993, *Reengineering the Corporation: A Manifesto for Business Revolution*, Nicholas Brealey Publishing.

Page 5: *The three most important things* – Alan Mitchell, 'Beyond the bottom line', *World Link Magazine*.

Page 7: *McGregor's classic book* – Douglas McGregor, 1960, *The Human Side of Enterprise*, McGraw-Hill.

Page 7: *The image of the worker* – James N Baron, 1988, 'The employment relation as a social relation', *Journal of the Japanese and International Economies*, 2, p 494.

Page 9: Levi-Strauss' management beliefs are shown in Jeffrey Pfeffer, 1994, *Competitive Advantage through People*, Harvard Business School Press.

Page 10: *The productivity revolution* – Peter F Drucker, 1991, 'The new productivity challenge', *Harvard Business Review*, Nov–Dec, pp 69–79.

Page 12: *Writ large, that sort of attitude* – Charles Handy, 1995, 'Trust and the virtual organization', *Harvard Business Review*, May–June, pp 39–49.

Page 14: *Our management information* – H Thomas Johnson, 1989, *Activity Management and Performance Measurement in a Service Organization*, Proceedings of 1989 Symposium.

Chapter 2

Page 21: *Given that change is inevitable* – Gary Hamel and CK Pralahad, 1994, 'Competing for the future', *Harvard Business Review*, Jul–Aug, pp 122–8.

Page 23: *large American organisations* – reported in the *Financial Times*, 20 March 1994.

Page 25: *Recent evidence casts doubt* – surveys by the Cresap division of Towers Perrin, cited in Anne Fisher, 'Morale Crisis', *Fortune*, 18 November 1991, pp 71–2.

Page 25: *The performance improvement efforts* – Robert H Schaffer and Harvey A Thomson, 1992, 'Successful change programs begin with results', *Harvard Business Review*, Jan-Feb, pp 80–9.

Page 25: *rollercoaster travelling through time* – Michael D Shields and S Mark Young, 1992, 'Effective long-term cost reduction: A strategic perspective', *Journal of Cost Management*, Spring.

Page 26: *Management at General Motors* – 'Rumble in Buick City', *Business Week*, 10 October 1994.

Pages 27–8: The Digital case study is drawn from articles in the *Financial Times*, 26 July 1994 and *Business Week*, 19 June 1995.

Pages 28–9: The Compaq case study is drawn from an article in the *Financial Times*, 25 July 1994.

Pages 29–30: The Sears case study is drawn from Leonard A Schlesinger and James L Heskett, 1991, 'The service-driven service company', *Harvard Business Review*, Sept–Oct, pp 71–81.

Page 31: *Federal Express is another startling success story* – drawn from 'Debate: How does service drive the service company?', *Harvard Business Review*, Nov–Dec 1991.

Page 35: *The budget is the bane of corporate America* – article in *Fortune*, 29 May 1995.

Page 35: *The authors of a recent CAM-I report – A Journey to Advanced Management System: A Report on the Research and Findings of the CAM-I Advanced Budgeting Group*, CAM-I Inc, September 1994.

Page 36: *We realised that our business planning system* – article in *The Economist*, 19 November 1994.

Page 36: *Thanks to new technologies* – J B Quinn, T L Doorley and P C Pacquette, 1990, 'Beyond products: Services based strategy', *Harvard Business Review*, Mar–Apr, pp 58–67.

Page 36: *The Boston Consulting Group* – quoted in the *Sloan Management Review*, Summer 1994, p 52.

Page 44: *We found that even the most advanced companies – A Journey to Advanced Management System: A Report on the Research and Findings of the CAM-I Advanced Budgeting Group*, CAM-I Inc, September 1994.

Chapter 3

Page 46: *Many people who have studied* – H Thomas Johnson, 1989, *Activity Management and Performance Measurement in a Service Organization*, Proceedings of 1989 Symposium.

Page 47: *Researchers claim that most organisations* – Jim Rigby, 1994, 'Activity based costing and process re-engineering at Hewlett Packard', in Bernard Taylor (ed), *Successful Change Strategies*, Director Books.

Page 48: *Fast cycle time* – Christopher Meyer, 1993, *Fast Cycle Time*, Free Press.

Page 50: *the linked set of value-creating activities* – John K Shank and Vijay Govindarajan, 1993, *Strategic Cost Management*, Free Press.

Page 51: *Turney has noted* – Peter B B Turney, 1992, 'Activity-based management', *Management Accounting*, January.

Page 51: *In a recent study* – from an ABM study carried out by David Hooper for Hewlett-Packard (UK) Ltd in 1992.

Page 52: *This is not job enrichment* – Peter F Drucker, 1991, 'The new productivity challenge', *Harvard Business Review*, Nov–Dec, p 74.

Page 52: *hidden factory* – Jeffrey G Miller and Thomas E Vollmann, 1985, 'The hidden factory', *Harvard Business Review*, Sept–Oct, pp 142–51.

Page 53–5: The GE case study is draen from James P Womack and Daniel T Jones, 1994, 'From lean production to the lean enterprise', *Harvard Business Review*, Mar–Apr, pp 93–103.

Page 56–7: The Process Plus case study is from William I Zingwill, 1993, *Lightning Strategies for Innovation*, Lexington Books.

Page 59: *starting over* – Michael Hammer and James Champy, 1993, *Reengineering the Corporation: A Manifesto for Business Revolution*, Nicholas Brealey Publishing.

Page 59: The Ford case study is drawn from Michael Hammer, 1990, 'Reengineering work: Don't automate, obliterate', *Harvard Business Review*, Jul–Aug, pp 104–12.

Page 62: *the company's performance was the result* – report in the *Financial Times*, 11 January 1994.

Page 64: *a number of reasons why ABM projects fail* – R Steven Player and David E Keys, 1995, 'Lessons from the ABM battlefield: Getting off to the right start', *Journal of Cost Management*, Spring, pp 26–33.

Chapter 4

Page 73: *Achieving competitive success through people* – Jeffrey Pfeffer, 1994, *Competitive Advantage through People*, Harvard Business School Press.

Page 74: *Jeffrey Pfeffer, for example, offers powerful evidence* – Jeffrey Pfeffer, 1994, *Competitive Advantage through People*, Harvard Business School Press.

Page 74: *When most companies reorganise* – Robert Howard, 1992, 'The CEO as organizational architect: An interview with Xerox's Paul Allaire', *Harvard Business Review*, Sept–Oct, pp 107–21.

Page 75: *Bottom-up empowerment* – H Thomas Johnson, 1992, 'It's time to stop overselling activity-based concepts', *Management Accounting*, Sept.

Page 76: *People working together with integrity* – Brian Dumaine, 1994, 'Mr Learning Organization', *Fortune*, 17 October.

Pages 78–9: The GEG case study is drawn from an article in *McKinsey Quarterly* by Frank Ostroff and Douglas Smith, 1992 No 1.

Page 79: *In the two years since* – from an article in *McKinsey Quarterly* by Frank Ostroff and Douglas Smith, 1992 No 1.

Page 80: *The order management cycle* – Benson P Shapiro, V Kasturi Rangan and John J Sviolka, 1992, 'Staple yourself to an order', *Harvard Business Review*, Jul–Aug, pp 113–22.

Page 81: *In the post-industrial age* – Michael Hammer and James Champy, 1993, *Reengineering the Corporation: A Manifesto for Business Revolution,* Nicholas Brealey Publishing.

Page 81: *By eliminating unnecessary steps* – James P Womack and Daniel T Jones, 1994, 'From lean production to the lean enterprise', *Harvard Business Review*, Mar–Apr, pp 93–103.

Page 83: *It came as no shock* – Jim Rigby, 1994, 'Activity based costing and process re-engineering at Hewlett Packard', in Bernard Taylor (ed), *Successful Change Strategies*, Director Books.

Page 84: The information on Kodak, GE and Xerox is drawn from an article in *McKinsey Quarterly* by Frank Ostroff and Douglas Smith, 1992 No 1.

Page 85: *centres of excellence* – James P Womack and Daniel T Jones, 1994, 'From lean production to the lean enterprise', *Harvard Business Review*, Mar–Apr, pp 93–103.

Pages 86–7: The information on Milliken, Motorola, GE and Kodak is drawn from an article in *McKinsey Quarterly* by Frank Ostroff and Douglas Smith, 1992 No 1.

Page 88: *The surest way to destroy cooperation* – Alfie Kohn, 1993, 'Why incentive plans cannot work', *Harvard Business Review,* Sept–Oct.

Page 88: *The traditional financial mentality* – quoted in Jeffrey Pfeffer, 1994, *Competitive Advantage through People*, Harvard Business School Press.

Page 88–9: *James Champy has argued persuasively* – James Champy, 1994, 'Time to reengineer the manager', *Financial Times*, 14 January.

Page 89: *Under the new work structures* – quoted in Jeffrey Pfeffer, 1994, *Competitive Advantage through People*, Harvard Business School Press.

Page 90: *there is a great deal of talk today* – Peter F Drucker, 1993, *Post Capitalist Society*, Butterworth-Heinemann.

Page 90: *At many companies* – Christopher Meyer, 1994, 'How the right measures help teams excel', *Harvard Business Review*, May–June, pp 95–103.

Page 91: *We will win and you will lose* – quoted in Jeffrey Pfeffer, 1994, *Competitive Advantage through People*, Harvard Business School Press.

Page 91: *Pfeffer has argued equally strongly* – Jeffrey Pfeffer, 1994, *Competitive Advantage through People*, Harvard Business School Press.

Page 93: *After nine years of working together* – Gerald D Radford, 1994, 'Establishing a high-performance work culture: Merging British and Japanese approaches, in Bernard Taylor (ed), *Successful Change Strategies*, Director Books.

Page 93: *Bain & Co have shown* – Rahul Jacob, 1994, 'Why some customers are more equal than others', *Fortune*, 19 September.

Page 93: *Evidence from the Marriott hotel group* – Leonard A Schlesinger and James L Heskett, 1991, 'The service-driven service company', *Harvard Business Review,* Sept–Oct, pp 71–81.

Chapter 5

Page 95: *What you measure is what you get* – Robert S Kaplan and David P Norton, 1992, 'The balanced scorecard: Measures that drive performance', *Harvard Business Review*, Jan–Feb, pp 71–9.

Page 96: *Understanding the strengths* – Joseph Fisher, 1992, 'Use of nonfinancial performance measures', *Journal of Cost Management*, Spring.

Page 97: *Historically we have tended* – quoted in Alan Mitchell, 'Beyond the bottom line', *World Link*.

Page 97: *Companies should focus on goals that matter* – H Thomas Johnson, 1992, 'It's time to stop overselling activity based concepts', *Management Accounting*, September, pp 26–35.

Page 98: *Many managers fail to understand* – 'A smarter way to manufacture', *Business Week*, 30 April 1990, pp 110–17.

Page 99: *Learning is no longer a separate activity* – Shoshana Zuboff, 1988, *In the Age of the Smart Machine: The Future of Work and Power*, Basic Books.

Page 100: *balacned scorecard* – Robert S Kaplan and David P Norton, 1992, 'The balanced scorecard: Measures that drive performance', *Harvard Business Review*, Jan–Feb, pp 71–9.

Page 102: The information on Rockwater is taken from a Harvard Business School case study prepared by Robert S Kaplan, 9-190-061, rev. 7.12.91.

Page 102: *You ask if we spend too much time* – quoted in Alan Mitchell, 'Beyond the bottom line', *World Link*.

Page 102: *On taking over at IBM* – *Business Week*, 7 February 1994, p 49.

Page 102: The information on Arthur Andersen is drawn from Alan Mitchell, 'Beyond the bottom line', *World Link*.

Page 103–105: The information on ADI is taken from a Harvard Business School case study prepared by Robert S Kaplan, 9-190-061, rev. 7.12.91.

Page 107: *Benchmarking is not industrial tourism* – N M Tichy and Ram Charan, 1995, 'The CEO as coach: An interview with Allied Signal's Lawrence A Bossidy', *Harvard Business Review*, Mar–Apr, pp 69–78.

Page 107: *In 1981 Xerox launched a recovery programme* – Robert Howard, 1992, 'The CEO as organizational architect: An interview with Xerox's Paul Allaire", *Harvard Business Review*, Sept–Oct, pp 107–21.

Page 108: *typically undermine the very processes* – Alfie Kohn, 1993, 'Why incentive plans cannot work', *Harvard Business Review,* Sept–Oct.

Page 109: *corporate staff groups* – 'Implementing the balanced scorecard at FMC Corporation: An interview with Larry D Brady', *Harvard Business Review*, Sept–Oct 1993.

Page 110: *The inability to quantify changes* – Joseph Fisher, 1992, 'Use of nonfinancial performance measures', *Journal of Cost Management*, Spring.

Page 111: *Is there a point* – Robert G Eccles and Philip J Pyburn, 1992, 'Creating a comprehensive system to measure performance', *Management Accounting*, October.

Page 112: *The team and senior managers* – Christopher Meyer, 1994, 'How the right measures help teams excel', *Harvard Business Review*, May–June, pp 95–103.

Page 113: *The bureaucracy routinely emasculated* – Robert S Kaplan and David P Norton, 1992, 'The balanced scorecard: Measures that drive performance', *Harvard Business Review*, Jan–Feb, pp 71–9.

Page 115: *Until a business returns a profit* – Peter F Drucker, 1995, 'The information executives truly need', *Harvard Business Review*, Jan–Feb.

Chapter 6

Page 116: *Many enterprises* – M Bromwich and A Bhimani, 1994, *Management Accounting Pathways to Progress*, CIMA.

Page 119: *We've been brought up to manage* – Jeffrey G Miller and Thomas E Vollmann, 1985, 'The hidden factory', *Harvard Business Review*, Sept–Oct, pp 142–51.

Page 119: *Miller and Vollman have suggested* – Jeffrey G Miller and Thomas E Vollmann, 1985, 'The hidden factory', *Harvard Business Review*, Sept–Oct, pp 142–51.

Page 120: *At the end of the assembly line* – James P Womack and Daniel T Jones, 1994, 'From lean production to the lean enterprise', *Harvard Business Review*, Mar–Apr, pp 93–103.

Page 120: *According to Stalk* – George Stalk Jr, 1988, 'Time: The next source of competitive advantage', *Harvard Business Review*, Jul–Aug, pp 41–51.

Page 120: *born of the need to make* – George Stalk Jr, 1988, 'Time: The next source of competitive advantage', *Harvard Business Review*, Jul–Aug, pp 41–51.

Page 121: *Douglas Shinsato* – quoted in Ford S Worthy, 1991, 'Japan's smart secret weapon', *Fortune*, 12 August.

Page 121: The information on Bellcore is taken from Edward J Kovac and Henry P Troy, 1989, 'Getting transfer prices right: What Bellcore did', *Harvard Business Review*, Sept–Oct.

Page 123: *I understand as well as you* – John Shank, 1990, 'Contribution margin analysis: No longer rele- vant/Strategic cost management: The new paradigm', *Journal of Management Accounting Research*, Vol 2, Fall.

Page 123: *Now the only way* – Peter F Drucker, 1963, *Harvard Business Review.*

Page 124: *Aldi suggests* – Hamdi F Aldi, 1994, 'A multicontribution activity-based income statement, *Journal of Cost Management*, Fall.

Page 124: *Although simplistic product costing methods* – H Thomas Johnson and Robert S Kaplan, 1987, *Relevance Lost: The Rise and Fall of Management Accounting*, Harvard Business School Press.

Page 124: *If only one person* – Robin Cooper and Robert S Kaplan, 1991, *The Design of Cost Management Systems*, Prentice-Hall International.

Page 126: *The purpose of cost driver accounting* – Robin Cooper and Peter B B Turney, 1990, 'Internally focused activity-based cost systems', in Robert S Kaplan (ed), *Measures for Manufacturing Decisions*, Harvard Business School Press.

Page 127: *Drucker suggests* – Peter F Drucker, 1995, 'The information executives truly need', *Harvard Business Review*, Jan–Feb, pp 54–62.

Page 128: *Current evidence and experience* – M Bromwich and A Bhimani, 1994, *Management Accounting Pathways to Progress*, CIMA.

Page 128: *Ness and Cacuzza estimate* – Joseph A Ness and Thomas G Cacuzza, 1995, 'Tapping the full poten- tial of ABC', *Harvard Business Review*, Jul–Aug.

Page 128: *Our exposure to some 20 organisations* – Nanni, Dixon and Vollmann, 1992, 'Redesigning manage- ment accounting for strategic management', *Journal of Accounting Research*, Fall.

Page 131: *Mercedes now has to produce* – interview in *Business Week*, 4 July 1994.

Pages 131–2: The information on Toyota is taken from an article by Rajan R Kamath and Jeffrey K Liker, 1994, 'A second look at Japanese product development', *Harvard Business Review*, Nov–Dec.

Page 132: *They taught me to concentrate* – quoted in William L Zangwill, 1993, *Lightning Strategies for Innovation*, Lexington Books.

Page 134: *The provision and analysis of financial information* – M Bromwich and A Bhimani, 1994, *Management Accounting Pathways to Progress*, CIMA.

Page 136: *Womack and Jones* – James P Womack and Daniel T Jones, 1994, 'From lean production to the lean enterprise', *Harvard Business Review*, Mar–Apr, pp 93–103.

Page 138: *This failure to listen* – Francis J Gouillart and Frederick D Sturdivant, 1994, 'Spend a day in the life of your customers', *Harvard Business Review*, Jan–Feb, pp 116–25.

Page 138: *One of the things we are starting to understand* – M Hergert and D Morris, 'Accounting data for value chain analysis', *Strategic Management Journal*, 10, pp 175–88.

Page 138: *attempts to control costs...may be futile* – M C Burnstein, 1988, *Life Cycle Costing in Cost Accounting for the '90s: Responding to Technological Change*, National Association of Accountants, p 261.

Page 139: *The manufacturing cycle for a car* – Christopher Meyer, 1993, *Fast Cycle Time*, Free Press.

Page 141: *We were able to tell engineers* – Jim Rigby, 1994, 'Activity based costing and process re-engineer- ing at Hewlett Packard', in Bernard Taylor (ed), *Successful Change Strategies*, Director Books.

Chapter 7

Page 142: *It is common for a business* – Frederick F Reichheld and W Earl Sasser Jr, 1990, 'Zero defections: Quality comes to services, *Harvard Business Review*, Sept–Oct, 105–111.

Page 143: *To achieve competitive and profitable operations* – H Thomas Johnson, 1992, 'It's time to stop over- selling activity-based concepts', *Management Accounting*, Sept.

Page 143: *Activity analysis has shown* – Robin Bellis-Jones, 1989, 'Customer profitability analysis', *Management Accounting*, February.

Page 143: *for similar transactions can be as much as 30 per cent* – Elliot B Ross, 1984, 'Making money with proactive pricing', *Harvard Business Review*, Nov–Dec, p 145.

Page 143: *Myer has suggested* – Randy Myer, 1989, 'Manage your customers', *Harvard Business Review*, Nov–Dec.

Page 144: The pharmaceutical distribution company study is taken from George Foster, 1994, *Using and Moving Beyond First Generation Customer Profitability Reports*, CIMA Research Paper, January, No 2, and Robert S Kaplan, Harvard Business School Case 9-190-002, rev 27.7.89.

Page 144: The Kanthal case study is taken from Robin Cooper and Robert S Kaplan, 1991, *The Design of Cost Management Systems,* Prentice-Hall International.

Page 146: The distributor study is taken from a Develin & Partners booklet on *Activity-Based Cost Management,* 1990.

Page 146: The American building supplies company case is taken from Robin Cooper and Robert S Kaplan, 1988, 'Measure costs right: Make the right decisions', *Harvard Business Review,* Sept–Oct.

Page 150: *Anderson and Narus allude to this –* James C Anderson and James A Narus, 1995, 'Capturing the value of supplementary services', *Harvard Business Review,* Jan–Feb, pp 75–83.

Page 150: *It's management by anecdote –* Benson P Shapiro, V Kasturi Rangan, Rowland T Moriarty and Elliot B Ross, 1987, 'Manage customers for profits (not just sales)', *Harvard Business Review,* Sept–Oct.

Page 150: *Robin Bellis-Jones has pointed out –* Robin Bellis-Jones, 1989, 'Customer profitability analysis', *Management Accounting,* February.

Page 150: *Anderson and Narus point out –* James C Anderson and James A Narus, 1995, 'Capturing the value of supplementary services', *Harvard Business Review,* Jan–Feb, pp 75–83.

Page 151: *I think that an unquestioned belief –* Robert S Kaplan, 1992, 'In defense of activity-based cost management', *Management Accounting,* Nov.

Page 152: *Studies by Bain & Co –* Rahul Jacob, 1994, 'Why some customers are more equal than others', *Fortune,* 19 Sept.

Page 154: *By the year end –* from an article in *Fortune,* 3 April 1995.

Page 155: *The links in the chain –* James L Heskett, Thomas O Jones, Gary W Loveman, W Earl Sasser Jr and Leonard A Schlesinger, 1994, 'Putting the service–profit chain to work', *Harvard Business Review,* Mar–Apr, pp 164–74.

Page 155: *Reichheld and Sasser have suggested –* Frederick F Reichheld and W Earl Sasser Jr, 1990, 'Zero defections: Quality comes to services', *Harvard Business Review,* Sept–Oct, pp 105–111.

Page 156: *Increase it, and a beneficial flywheel effect kicks in –* Rahul Jacob, 1994, 'Why some customers are more equal than others', *Fortune,* 19 Sept.

Page 157: *Research on customer loyalty in the service sector –* Leonard A Schlesinger and James L Heskett, 1991, 'The service-driven service company', *Harvard Business Review,* Sept–Oct, pp 71–81.

Page 157: *The retention of customers –* Robert Ayling, 1991, *Harvard Business Review,* Nov–Dec.

Page 157: *Xerox has gone further than most –* James L Heskett, Thomas O Jones, Gary W Loveman, W Earl Sasser Jr and Leonard A Schlesinger, 1994, 'Putting the service–profit chain to work', *Harvard Business Review,* Mar–Apr, pp 164–74.

Page 158: *In the case of a large sportswear manufacturer –* Harvey N Shycon, 1992, 'Improved customer service: Measuring the payoff', *Journal of Business Strategy,* Jan–Feb.

Page 158: *In the case of a plastic laminates manufacturer –* Harvey N Shycon, 1991, 'Measuring the payoff from improved customer service', *Arthur D Little,* First Quarter.

Page 158: *Data collected by the US Department of Consumer Affairs –* Leonard A Schlesinger and James L Heskett, 1991, 'The service-driven service company', *Harvard Business Review,* Sept–Oct, pp 71–81.

Page 160: *A 1991 study –* James L Heskett, Thomas O Jones, Gary W Loveman, W Earl Sasser Jr and Leonard A Schlesinger, 1994, 'Putting the service–profit chain to work', *Harvard Business Review,* Mar–Apr, pp 164–74.

Page 160: *$2.5 million in commission income –* James L Heskett, Thomas O Jones, Gary W Loveman, W Earl Sasser Jr and Leonard A Schlesinger, 1994, 'Putting the service–profit chain to work', *Harvard Business Review,* Mar–Apr, pp 164–74.

Page 160: *The growing body of data –* Leonard A Schlesinger and James L Heskett, 1991, 'The service-driven service company', *Harvard Business Review,* Sept–Oct, pp 71–81.

Page 161: *One exception is Taco Bell –* James L Heskett, Thomas O Jones, Gary W Loveman, W Earl Sasser Jr and Leonard A Schlesinger, 1994, 'Putting the service–profit chain to work', *Harvard Business Review,* Mar–Apr, pp 164–74.

Page 161: *results for customers higher than anything else –* James L Heskett, Thomas O Jones, Gary W Loveman, W Earl Sasser Jr and Leonard A Schlesinger, 1994, 'Putting the service–profit chain to work', *Harvard Business Review,* Mar–Apr, pp 164–74.

Page 161: *Ritz-Carlton Hotel Co –* 'Why some customers are more equal than others', *Fortune,* 19 September 1994.

Page 162: *We've learned that a service rep –* from 'Debate: How does service drive the service company?', *Harvard Business Review,* Nov–Dec.

Chapter 8

Page 163: *Management accountants need to change* – Toshiro Hiromoto, 1991, 'Restoring the relevance of management accounting', *Journal of Management Accounting Research*, Vol 3, Fall.

Chapter 9

Page 193: *Most corporations are like giant jellies* – Richard Heygate, 1993, 'Immoderate redesign', *McKinsey Quarterly*, No 1.

Page 194: *Catching up is not enough* – Gary Hamel and CK Pralahad, 1994, 'Competing for the future', *Harvard Business Review*, Jul–Aug, pp 122–8.

Page 194: *The right conversation is essential* – 'Memo to a CEO by Steven F Dichter, Chris Gagnon and Ashok Alexander, *McKinsey Quarterly*, Spring 1993.

Page 195: *The command and control organisation* – Peter F Drucker, 1995, 'The information executives truly need', *Harvard Business Review*, Jan–Feb, pp 54–62.

Page 195: *At chemical firm Process Plus* – William L Zangwill, 1993, *Lightning Strategies for Innovation*, Lexington Books.

Page 196: *Charles Handy has suggested* – Charles Handy, 1995, 'Trust and the virtual organization', *Harvard Business Review*, May–June, pp 39–49.

Page 196: *The concept of membership* – Charles Handy, 1995, 'Trust and the virtual organization', *Harvard Business Review*, May–June, pp 39–49.

Page 197: *The 'new style' head office* – 'Redesigning the head office at BP Oil', in Bernard Taylor (ed), 1994, *Successful Change Strategies,* Director Books.

Page 197: *At Lincoln Electric* – quoted in Jeffrey Pfeffer, 1994, *Competitive Advantage through People*, Harvard Business School Press.

Page 198: *Organisations can perform well* – 'Memo to a CEO by Steven F Dichter, Chris Gagnon and Ashok Alexander, *McKinsey Quarterly*, Spring 1993.

Page 198: *We didn't know this was where we were going* – quoted in Jeffrey Pfeffer, 1994, *Competitive Advantage through People*, Harvard Business School Press.

Page 199: *All these moves have helped* – 'Managing radical change at the Automobile Association', in Bernard Taylor (ed), 1994, *Successful Change Strategies,* Director Books.

Page 199: *I believe that the only way effectively* – 'Restructuring and revitalising the TSB', in Bernard Taylor (ed), 1994, *Successful Change Strategies,* Director Books.

Page 200: *GM had no real production system* – quoted in Jeffrey Pfeffer, 1994, *Competitive Advantage through People*, Harvard Business School Press.

Page 202: *The difficulty of connecting* – Thomas A Stewart, 1994, 'How to lead a revolution', *Fortune*, 28 November.

Page 204: *This lack of focus was evident* – Robert H Schaffer and Harvey A Thomson, 1992, 'Successful change programs begin with results', *Harvard Business Review*, Jan–Feb, pp 80–89.

Page 207: *Information technology has a polarising effect* – Thomas H Davenport, 1994, 'Saving IT's soul: Human-centered information management', *Harvard Business Review*, Mar–Apr, pp 119–31.

Page 210: *people think in terms of stories, not facts* – 'Your company's most valuable asset: Intellectual capital', *Fortune*, 3 October 1994.

INDEX